Whatever Happened to the Human Mind?

E. L. MASCALL

Whatever Happened to the Human Mind?

Essays in Christian Orthodoxy

LONDON
SPCK

First published 1980
SPCK
Holy Trinity Church
Marylebone Road
London NW1 4DU

Typeset by
Malvern Typesetting Services
Printed in Great Britain by
Redwood Burn Limited
Trowbridge and Esher

ISBN 0 281 03754 X

TO THE PRIESTS AND PEOPLE OF
SAINT MARY'S IN PIMLICO
WHO FOR MANY YEARS
HAVE PROVIDED THIS GRATEFUL AUTHOR
WITH AN ALTAR AND A HOME

Passer invenit sibi domum et turtur nidum sibi, ubi ponat pullos suos,
Altaria tua, Domine virtutum, rex meus et Deus meus.
Beati qui habitant in domo tua, Domine! In saecula saeculorum laudabunt te.

Contents

Acknowledgements

Thanks are due to the following for permission to quote from copyright sources:

Herder AG, Freiburg im Breisgau: 'God-World Relationship' by Waltern Kern in *Sacramentum Mundi*.

Cambridge University Press: *The Origin of Christology* by C. F. D. Moule.

Darton, Longman & Todd Ltd and The Westminster Press: *The Openness of Being* by E. L. Mascall.

David Higham Associates Ltd: Dante's *Divine Comedy*, translated by Dorothy L. Sayers and published by Penguin Books Ltd.

Longman Group Ltd: *Christian Theology and Natural Science* by E. L. Mascall.

Dr C. F. D. Moule: An excerpt from his book *The Phenomenon of the New Testament*, published by SCM Press Ltd.

Oxford University Press: *God as Spirit* by G. W. H. Lampe.

The Trustees of Katharine Farrer deceased: *The Glass of Vision* by Austin Farrer.

Foreword

The first four chapters of this book may be considered as essays in defence, illustration, and amplification of the plea which I made towards the end of 1977, in a volume entitled *Theology and the Gospel of Christ*, for a recovery among Anglicans of Christian theology in the strict and classical sense of 'the Science of God', as a living and growing intellectual activity organically rooted in the Christian tradition and consciously operating within the worshipping and redemptive community which is the Body of Christ. To this extent, therefore, this book is a sequel to the earlier one, in spite of its incomplete and un-systematic character. I believe that these topics are all of them important and urgent, though I recognize that there are others of equal importance and urgency with which I have not dealt; space and competence are both limited, *non omnia possumus omnes*. I have said nothing, for instance, about the burning question of the Church's concern with the social and political order. I would, however, emphasize that its satisfactory hand-ling requires a clear and coherent understanding of the Christian doctrines about God, Christ, man, and redemption which are logically and theologically antecedent to it and which are the subject of the central chapters of this book. It is precisely their weakness at this fundamental level that, in my opinion, accounts both for that reduction of Christianity to mere politics which Dr Edward Norman, in his recent Reith Lectures, has rightly diagnosed as the perpetual temptation of the con-temporary ecumenical movement and also Dr Norman's own inability to make any theological discrimination or judgement on social and political issues at all. Equally striking is the al-most complete lack of concern in academic theological circles with the explosively vigorous Liberation Theology of Latin America. Much of this is, I believe, open to serious theological criticism, especially as regards its Christology, and unless it receives and responds to this criticism its future as a movement of *Christian* renewal seems extremely hazardous. It is however evident that it is not likely to receive that kind of constructive criticism that is needed from our contemporary theological liberalism, which simply does not possess the necessary criteria *at the basic theological level*. Those criteria are, I believe, to be found in the traditional Chalcedonian Christology, which has unexplored depths and undeveloped potentialities whose very existence has hardly been recognized. I have given no explicit discussion of Liberation Theology in the present book; nevertheless I believe that the central chapters are basically about it—and about a number of other pressing issues besides.

A special word may be needed about the first chapter, which otherwise may seem out of place in a theological work. I believe that the theological relativism which has become such a prominent feature of the present day, so that, for example, instead of asking 'Has God become man?', we are told that we ought only to investigate whether the incarnation-myth provides a useful model for twentieth-century religious experience, is partly produced and partly encouraged by the corrosion of the notion of truth as the conformity of mind with reality, and that this in turn is connected with a radical scepticism about mind itself. Both philosophy and theology have been pervaded by it in one or another of its many forms, and those who are seduced by it are undeterred by the fact that in the very act of stating it they find themselves obliged to deny it. It may take a very blatant form, as in Dr Leslie Dewart's historical relativism, for which 'truth is not the adequacy of our representative operations, but the adequacy of our conscious existence';[1] it may take a less obvious form in Dr Wolfhart Pannenberg's notion of 'the ontological priority of the future', according to which statements about truth or falsehood can apparently be made only at the Last Day even if they are about events occurring before,[2] so that truth itself becomes an eschatological concept. This issue is not to be dodged by making remarks about the contrast between the Greek and the Jewish notion of truth and rejecting the former as un-biblical and intellectualistic. Not even the most hardened Thomist will hold that we are saved by intellect alone, by a *fides caritate non formata*; but to expound an allegedly biblical notion of faith and truth which not merely transcends but rejects the conformity of mind with reality is to render one's whole exposition incoherent and unintelligible. It is to reduce both preaching and theology to the level of that uninterpreted glossolalia which St Paul condemned as time-wasting and self-indulgent.

The final chapter took its origin in a different source from the others, namely an essay entitled 'Some Basic Considerations' which I contributed to a symposium on the ordination of women to the priesthood.[3] While finding the arguments against such ordination quite convincing, I was also brought to recognize that there are certain logically and theologically antecedent questions about the significance and relation of the two sexes in the orders of both creation and redemption which have never been fully investigated but whose clarification is urgently necessary if women are to find their proper place and dignity in the Church and are not to be fobbed off with a spurious masculinity. I have therefore attempted to make what can at best be only a preliminary essay in this field, in the hope that others may be able to follow it up more fully and adequately. The obvious starting point seemed to be the distinct roles played by the two sexes in the Incarnation, as that is understood in Christian tradition. That God is incarnate as a male and that his only human parent is a female, that is the one clearly revealed fact about the differentiation of the sexes in the order of redemption, and starting from it I have tried to see how on the one hand it relates to what empirical science shows about their differentiation in the natural order of creation and what on the other hand it suggests about the character of deity itself. This inevitably involves a good deal of speculation, and I am fully aware that the element of speculation increases as one works back from the Incarnate Son to his divine Person and thence to the tripersonal deity of Father, Son, and Spirit; our language and concepts become steadily more analogical as we proceed. Nevertheless it seems clear that there must be some factor of continuity unless we are to see the divine dispensation as involving sheer arbitrary gaps. I would therefore hope that this discussion might be considered on its merits and not as a covert polemic either for or against the ordination of women to the priesthood.

Finally I would say that, while I welcome the descriptions of my theological stance as orthodox and traditional, as stressing the permanent truth and vitality of the Christian revelation, I would reject the epithets 'conservative' and 'revolutionary', as indicating a merely subjective prejudice against or in favour of change as such. What I find impressive and exciting about traditional theological orthodoxy is its capacity for bringing out of its treasury previously unsuspected riches as the changing

circumstances of the Church and the world need them; I hope
that the chapter on Christology in the present volume provides
an illustration of this remarkable vitality and fertility, though it
cannot do more than indicate some of the areas that demand
attention. And as he tries in humility and loyalty to carry out
the particular tasks that have fallen to him, the theologian must
never forget that, essential as it is, the tradition of learning and
teaching—the intellectual tradition—which is his special
concern is only one strand and aspect of the great Tradition
which is nothing less than the living Christ himself in the Spirit-
filled Body the Church, within which his own life and thought
must be set. As Kenneth Leech has written:

> The gulf between 'academic' theology and the exercise of
> pastoral care and spiritual guidance has been disastrous for
> all concerned. . . . The study of theology, or at least of
> Christian theology, cannot survive in a healthy state apart
> from the life of prayer and the search for holiness. The
> theologian is essentially a man of prayer. . . . Theology is an
> encounter with the living God, not a detached academic
> exercise.[4]

1 *Man and His Mind:*
The Defence of the Intellectual Principle

Nolite fieri sicut equus et mulus, quibus non est intellectus
Ps. 31.9

WHATEVER HAPPENED TO THE HUMAN MIND?

By 'the Intellectual Principle' I do not intend anything esoteric or technical, but something which to the unsophisticated man or woman will probably seem so obvious as hardly to need stating, let alone defending, but which has nevertheless been widely called in question in the modern world, either implicitly or explicitly, by many philosophers and theologians, in spite of the fact that even to question it involves a tacit recognition of its truth. I mean by it the doctrine that the human mind, simply as mind, as *mens*, *intellectus*, *Geist*, or spirit, in contrast to lifeless beings and sub-human animals, is capable (*a*) of knowing truth and (*b*) of apprehending realities other than itself—not perfectly, exhaustively or infallibly but nevertheless authentically—and of correcting its own errors. This capacity is both complex and mysterious, not least because of the mind's embodied condition, a condition moreover which is not that of a pure spirit temporarily, or even permanently, constrained to function within a material mechanism having no special affinity or conformity to it, but is that of a very special kind of spirit whose normal situation is to be involved with a material body, and not just with any human body that happens to be available but with one which is uniquely adapted to it. It is this inherently body-correlated aspect of human mentality that has been expressed in the scholastic aphorisms that 'there is nothing in the intellect that was not first in a sense' (*nihil in intellectu quod non fuit prius in sensu*) and that 'the mind turns towards sensory images' (*mens convertit se ad phantasmata*), while on the other hand its fundamental spirituality is emphasized by the complementary affirmation that 'the mind can in some way become all things, not entitatively but intentionally' (*mens quodammodo fit omnia, non entitative sed intentionaliter*); and it is important to notice that the qualifying phrase, *non*

1

entitative sed intentionaliter, is concerned not to minimize or to reduce to metaphorical status the power of the mind to 'become other things' but to emphasize it. Although the mind cannot become other things 'entitatively', it really and truly can become them 'intentionally', that is by *stretching out into them*. 'Intention' in this context goes far beyond its everyday connotation of a mere aspiration or a registration of a future volition; in Latin, *intendere* is *tendere in*. This is undoubtedly very mysterious, but it is precisely what is involved in being a mind, in being spirit, and not a lump of lifeless matter or a brute beast. To be a spiritual being, even an embodied one, is to be able to penetrate other beings to their ontological interior, or (to describe this from the complementary standpoint) to make them part of one's own being without violating their own entitative integrity. In M. Etienne Gilson's words, 'The thing I know becomes myself by my cognition of it, unless we prefer to say that I am becoming it through knowing it.'[1] If we lose grasp of this fundamental characteristic of human knowledge, either one of two diametrically opposed consequences is almost sure to follow. At the one extreme, on the basis of post-Newtonian physics, you will find yourself thinking of human beings as simply highly complicated material systems interacting with other material systems according to deterministic physical laws, and you will end up as we are today, in spite of the work of relativity and quantum theorists, with human perception conceived on the model of the impact of elastic bodies, and human thinking conceived on the model of the electronic computer. Alternatively, at the other extreme, on the basis of Cartesian philosophy, you will find yourself thinking of human beings as pure spirits enjoying a purely intra-mental life and you will be forced, as Descartes was, to construct elaborate arguments to convince yourself that anything exists outside your mind at all. Or, with the British empiricists, you may achieve the heroic paradox of combining the two extremes. And the easiest way of combining extremes is to persuade yourself that one of the extremes is, in spite of appearances, really the same as the other. Let us see how this works out, starting from the standpoint of the materialistic physicist.

If you think of the process of perceiving an object as analogous to receiving a blow from the object on the surface of your body, you will conclude, on consideration, that strictly speaking, you never perceived the object at all. What you did perceive, and all that you could perceive, was the shock which you received when the object collided with you. Indeed, you were making a quite unjustified assumption in speaking about the object as colliding with you; for, unless you had access to some occult source of information, how could you know the object even existed? You may have felt as if the impact was the impact of an object, but what you felt was the impact and not the object. The stars which I see when I look up at the night-sky under what scientists describe as the impact of light-quanta from Ursa Major may be just as subjective, just as lacking in extra-mental reality, as the stars which I see when I receive a different kind of impact from a cosh, or, more exactly, from what I describe as a cosh. The transition in thought is clear. I began by assuming that perception consisted in the purely external impact of an object upon a sensitive subject. Then I reflected that, the impact being purely external, the subject was not in fact aware of the object at all, but only of a disturbance in his mind which strangely felt as if it had come from an external object. Then I argued that the subject had no ground for supposing that there were any external objects at all or that perception consisted of anything more than the subject's awareness of its own mental states. Finally—although not many were prepared to take this final step—remembering that I was myself the only percipient through whose perceptions my own knowledge was derived, I might take the final step of deciding that I was the only subject in existence, and so, although, like one of Bertrand Russell's correspondents, I might be surprised that so few people could be found who held such a reasonable view,[2] I might end up as the complete solipsist.

Even the most mechanistic philosopher could hardly deny the existence of mind altogether; at the very least he needed his own mind as a factory and storehouse for his own theories, though he could try to assimilate mental activity to a chemical process, as in the celebrated dictum that the brain secretes thought as the liver secretes bile. What at least appeared to have been achieved was the segregation of mentality in microscopic enclosures where it had only minimal communication with the external world. As E. A. Burtt wrote, in Newton's system the world that people had thought themselves living in—a world rich with colour and sound, redolent with fragrance, filled with gladness, love and beauty, speaking everywhere of purposive harmony and creative ideals—was crowded now into minute corners in the brains of scattered organic beings. The really important world outside was a world hard, cold, colourless, silent, and dead: a world of quantity, a world of mathematically computable motions in mechanical regularity.[3]

This picture of the perceptual process has persisted almost, if not quite, to the present day. Mr G. J. Warnock, criticizing an early phase of Bertrand Russell, has written:

It seems to be almost an occupational disease of those who reflect on the human nervous system that they should picture us as somehow located inside our own heads—at the point, that is, on which all the elaborate and ramified nerves converge. The observer is represented as being confined to the centre of his own nervous system, at a point from which as it were connecting wires run out into the outside world. In that world, it appears, there occur certain events which transmit electrical impulses along these wires, and thus there occur signals at the centre of the system, at the point where the observer is imprisoned and anxiously watching. Such signals, strictly speaking, are all that he ever observes. He may be able—it is not clear how—to form some dim notion of the remote, 'external' world; conceivably, by careful inference, he may reach conclusions as to its character which stand some chance of being true. But all that he really observes is the succession of signals arriving at the inside end of his nervous network; and these, of course, are all 'in his brain'.[4]

Mr Warnock rightly described this picture as 'fantastical'. 'Our nervous systems,' he asserts, 'so far from forming a barrier between ourselves and the "external" world, in fact put us in touch (sometimes literally) with that world in the most direct of all possible ways; they are inside us, not we inside them.'[5] With this last comment the strictest Thomist would agree; for he would insist that the subject of perception and of thinking and willing is not just the soul but the whole man, and that the soul, so far from being confined to one point of the body is *tota in toto et tota in aliqua parte*.

I shall leave the present-day situation for the moment in order to see the real root of the trouble, and for this we must go back to the seventeenth and eighteenth centuries. And there we find an assumption, which is common to rationalists, idealists, and empiricists alike, as clear in Hume as it is in Berkeley, that what is apprehended by the mind in an act of perception—what scholasticism would call the *objectum quod*—is a sensible particular—a coloured shape, a low-pitched grunt, a painful jab and so on. This at least is sure, whatever else is uncertain. Whether anything lies beyond it, and, if so, what the nature of that may be, is a matter of assumption, deduction, and/or speculation; and about this there is violent disagreement. What seems too obvious to dispute is that perception is primarily sensation and that the sense-object—what will later be called the *sensum*, *sensibile*[6] or *sense-datum*, but would in the Middle Ages have been called the *sensible species*—is simply a modification of the mind and therefore is grasped by the mind infallibly and immediately.

For Descartes, each of the sense-objects—*idées-tableaux* as he called them, 'picture-ideas'—carried a kind of certificate guaranteeing that it was a faithful representation of an external reality. But certificates, as we know, can be forged, and it required the whole paraphernalia of the ontological arguments for the existence of God to convince Descartes that he was not being duped by a *malin génie*. For Locke, the sense-objects—his 'simple ideas'—are formed by the mind into complex ideas of substances as the substrata which uphold them. Since secondary qualities, such as colours and tastes, are incurably subjective, substances can be allowed only primary qualities such as size, shape, and motion; nevertheless, even in this etiolated condition, substances are known only inferentially, simple ideas are what we genuinely perceive. Berkeley, however, had no difficulty in showing that, given the basic assumption that perception is simply sensation (which he accepts no less than Locke), primary qualities are no less subjective than are secondary qualities; or, to speak more accurately, all qualities are in fact secondary. *Esse est percipi*, nothing can exist unless a mind is perceiving it; nevertheless, the world is a patterned order and not a spasmodic and unconnected chaos,

5

since God is, in the words of the limerick, 'always about in the quad'.

Hume was even more extreme in his mentalism. It is true that for him the mind itself was without any substantial or enduring character: 'what we call a *mind*', he wrote, 'is nothing but a heap or collection of different perceptions, united together by certain relations, and supposed, though falsely to be endowed with a perfect simplicity and identity.'[7] (Hume, of course, never appeared frankly to recognize that in a statement like this he was sawing off the branch on which a necessary and loquacious participant denoted as 'we' or 'I' was sitting throughout the treatise.) But this does not mean that the *objects* of perception were any more substantial or enduring than the subjects. Rather, it meant that both subject and object as enduring entities had vanished in a kind of psychological atomism; nothing existed except a dust of unconnected momentary acts of awareness, and in each of these the object was a simple impression or idea. 'Thus', wrote William Turner,

> did Hume complete the work of empiricism, Locke reasoned away everything except the primary qualities of bodies and the unknown substratum (substance) in which they adhere; Berkeley showed that even the substance and primary qualities of bodies might be reasoned away, and now Hume applies the same solvent to the substance of mind itself, and leaves nothing but phenomena.[8]

'Nothing but phenomena'—this might indeed seem to be the end of the road, and it is significant that several leading modern English philosophers of the dominant linguistic school have taken Hume as the only earlier philosopher with whom the philosophical neophyte of today need concern himself. This is interesting, in view of the fact that, by his own testimony, Hume found that his philosophizing reduced him to such a state of depression and desperation—'I . . . begin', he wrote, 'to fancy myself in the most deplorable condition imaginable, environed with the deepest darkness, and utterly deprived of the use of every member and faculty'[9]—that he could only recover his customary equilibrium and good-humour by laying aside his philosophy and spending three or four hours in dining, playing backgammon, conversing, and making merry with his friends. And indeed the practical result of the Humean influence has not been to produce a great popular movement proclaiming to the community at large with evangelical fervour the news that all our acts of perception are isolated experiences without continuity at either their subjective or objective poles; it has been to turn philosophy into an esoteric and specialized pursuit having little relevance to ordinary life. Even English linguistic philosophers speak and act, outside their strictly professional sphere, as if they were enduring intelligent beings enjoying a life of continuous mental and physical interaction with other enduring intelligent beings and enduring physical entities. Before considering further the present situation we must, however, take note of the massively influential figure of Immanuel Kant, whose *Critique of Pure Reason* appeared in 1781 and who, as he himself testified, was awakened from dogmatic slumber by David Hume. For Kant the basic problem raised by perception is this: starting from the phenomena which we experience, how can we distinguish those features of the objects which belong to them independently of the fact that we experience them from those features which we may have unconsciously and unintentionally imposed on them in the very act of experiencing them? Since all that we know is the completely cooked dish, how can we decide what it would be like if it had not been subjected to the process of cooking? How can we mentally uncook it, seeing that the cooking has been done by our minds? Kant's intimidatingly elaborate transcendental method is largely devoted to this question: how can we get to the *noöumenon*, the transcendental object, the thing-in-itself (the *Ding an sich*) that lies behind the phenomenon? It is not surprising that opinions differ as to his success, but as to his influence, both by attraction and by repulsion, on subsequent philosophizing there can be no doubt, though not many have expressed themselves as downrightly as Bertrand Russell:

> Kant deluged the philosophic world with muddle and mystery, from which it is only now beginning to emerge. Kant has the reputation of being the greatest of modern philosophers, but to my mind he was a mere misfortune.[10]

Russell was writing a half-century ago; some would doubt whether it has emerged yet! But, whether or not they would express themselves with the vigour of Russell, most Anglo-Saxon philosophers today would agree that with Kant the attempt to prove the existence of either an enduring subject or an enduring object of the perceptive act came to a well-deserved end; and, since neither philosophy nor any other technique could possibly succeed in this enterprise, some other task had to be found for philosophy to do. What could not possibly be denied was that philosophers, like other people, make use of words, and, from the time when Ludwig Wittgenstein's *Tractatus Logico-philosophicus* was published in 1919 and the 'Vienna Circle' began its brief and tragic career in the early nineteen-twenties down to the present day, philosophy in the English-speaking world has concentrated more and more upon the study of language. (On the European continent Wittgenstein and the Vienna Circle have had little permanent impact, and the flourishing movements of existentialism and phenomenology are rejected with contempt by most British philosophers as unrecognisable as philosophy at all.) Wittgenstein's 'logical atomism' envisaged language as purporting to picture a world of fact, though without any commitment as to the metaphysical status of that world, but Wittgenstein himself came to be convinced that it was inadequate.[11] Mr A. J. (now Sir Alfred) Ayer's 'logical positivism' limited the meaningfulness of language to its capacity to describe empirical sense-phenomena but, in spite of its author's ingenuity, it could never escape from the need to cut its own throat.[12] The linguistic movement in consequence tended to lose all concern with the question of meaning and, while allowing philosophers to widen their range of interest beyond empirically verifiable propositions and logical tautologies, so that ethical and even religious statements become once again worthy of attention, it restricted its investigations simply to their structure and to the conditions under which people whose linguistic behaviour included them uttered them; any question of their possible reference to extra-linguistic reality was ruled out as probably meaningless and certainly outside the legitimate business of philosophers. This orientation was characteristic of the later, in contrast with the earlier, Wittgenstein and, with the posthumous publication of his *Philosophical Investigations* in 1953 it spread beyond the esoteric group of the original disciples of the jealously guarded cult-figure into the outside world.[13] It is true that some recent writers have been cautious of committing themselves to a purely behavioural view of

language and of reducing philosophy merely to a study of the
linguistic habits of certain groups of persons and of the conditions under which certain types of utterance are made, but the
difficulties are very great. For if you are going to hold that
words are associated with objects—even purely phenomenal
objects—because those objects are what they *mean*, the
question arises as to whence they derive their meanings. You
may be able, though it will not be easy, to construct a theory of
meaning if you hold a Humean doctrine of the *objects* of
perception, but it will hardly be possible if you hold a Humean
doctrine of the *subjects*. Unless you can affirm that words
acquire their meanings from minds which use them you may be
forced into holding that words are a kind of self-subsistent
entity that generate their meanings for themselves. Such an
ontological verbalism, though some have claimed to find it in
the later writings of Martin Heidegger,[14] can hardly commend
itself to hard-headed British empiricists. But we ought not
perhaps to be surprised if it turns out to be difficult to make
intelligibility intelligible without believing in intelligence. In
such a situation of frustration the easy way out is to talk about
something else, and this is what in his later years Wittgenstein
did. 'Philosophy', he wrote, 'simply puts everything before us,
and neither explains nor deduces anything. Since everything lies
open to view there is nothing to explain.'[15] That many
distinguished and established philosophers, including some
who have helped to bring this situation about, are not entirely
happy about it is suggested by the impressive collection of
essays which Professor H. D. Lewis gathered together in 1963
under the title *Clarity is not Enough: Essays in Criticism of
Linguistic Philosophy*,[16] but fourteen years later the concern
with language seems still to be dominant. Even those
philosophers who have interested themselves in the notion of
'referring' have been reticent about the nature and status of the
relatum to which language refers. But now, after this brief,
breathless, and obviously incomplete[17] survey of the history and
present state of Anglo-Saxon philosophy, we must inquire how
it began and why it took the course it did.

The obvious starting-point is a human act of perception, and
there will be universal agreement that the object which is
perceived is in the mind that perceives it, even if we should have
to concede to Hume that this 'mind' exists only as long as the

act of perception. But does the object exist outside the mind as well? A medieval philosopher, or at any rate a Thomist, would have no doubt that it did, with certain exceptions for which he would give an explanation. But a sixteenth-century philosopher was not so sure. If he was Descartes he would admit that the object in his mind certainly purported to be a picture—a representation—of something outside, but he would be disturbed by the fear that he was being deluded by a mischievous sprite, a *malin génie*, and would need to be convinced by ontological arguments of the existence of a good God before this fear could be allayed. If, however, he was a British empiricist, his doubts would take a different form. For him, perception was, in its essence, simply sensation and its primary object was what we should now call a sense-datum—a coloured patch, a low-pitched grunt, a painful jab or whatever—and anything beyond that, any cause of it outside the mind, was a matter of assumption, deduction or speculation. Now sense-data are, as a matter of experience, very subjective; the colour of the patch, for instance, will depend upon my state of health, my immediately preceding visual experiences, drugs that I may have taken and so on. To suppose that the-patch-that-I-see exists when I am not seeing it would be to commit the philosophical crime of crude realism, than which few delinquencies are more reprehensible, and yet what ground have I for supposing that anything exists, either when I am or when I am not seeing it, except the-patch-that-I-see (and other sense data of similar status)? If I take refuge with Locke and say that at least the primary qualities of size, shape, and motion will be the same for all observers, Berkeley will be at hand to interject that that may be so but yet I know them only as ideas in my mind, and where except in a mind can ideas possibly be? If in desperation I take refuge with the physiologists and assert that the mechanism of my nervous system furnishes me with reliable information from the external world, I shall be told that this alleged mechanism and this so-called 'external world' themselves exist only 'in my mind' and that, even if it were granted for the sake of argument that the mechanism was what the materialists allege it to be, I cannot be sure that this information has reached me without distortion when it has come through this complicated process of coding, transmission, and decoding. And in any case, Hume will arrive at the end of the day to dissect my mind into its separate perceptual experiences, and I shall have nothing to rescue me from ultimate scepticism but dinner, conversation, and backgammon.

Now clearly something has gone wrong at the start, and no subsequent evasive action, however skilful and elaborate, can manage to undo its effects. The error was, I suggest, the simple identification of perception with sensation or, more precisely, the assumption that the sense-datum, *sensum*, *sensibile*, phenomenon, impression, idea, or sensible species—for to their different users these terms are virtually synonymous—is not merely the *objectum quo*, the medium or instrument, of the act of perception, but is its terminus, its *objectum quod*. On this assumption, any knowledge of external reality that was held to result from our perceptive experience could be due only to assumption, speculation, or deduction, all of which are in their different ways highly unreliable. The consequence of this was the gulf between physical scientists and philosophers which lasted until well into the present century. The physical scientists, who wanted above all to believe in a stable and regular material universe, bolstered up their Newtonian mechanics with a Cartesian doctrine of representative perception as naturalized by Locke. They wanted indeed an intelligible world, which would be amenable to treatment by mathematics, but they assumed that the intelligible structure of the real world must simply reduplicate the structure of the world of our sensible experience, with the so-called secondary qualities left out and a few mysterious non-sensible qualities, such as mass and electric charge, brought in; the intelligible world was essentially a sensible world, even if, paradoxically, we never sensed it.[18] On the other hand, philosophers, going beyond Locke to Hume, tended more and more to a purely phenomenalistic position, which eliminated the putative external world altogether, at least from the concern of philosophers, until, in a fear that this was the primrose path leading to mysticism and metaphysics, it was felt to be safer to confine oneself to the study of language. (The attempt, by some Cambridge men like Russell and C. D. Broad, to redefine physical objects as logical constructs of sense-data or sensibilia, while it appealed to those who were attempting a similar redefinition of the entities of mathematics, received little attention from the majority of British

11

philosophers, whose background tended to be that of Oxford Greats rather than that of the Mathematical Tripos.)

THE ROAD TO RECOVERY

What I would maintain we need is to recover the conviction that we are intelligent beings, embodied minds, living in an intelligible world, which we grasp not *by* but *through* our senses. That we are subject to error is a mere consequence of our finitude and disorder; we do not need an elaborate theory to explain it, and it is fortunate that, unless we are placed in very abnormal perceptual situations or are suffering from mental sickness, we are usually able to correct our mistakes. Intelligence does not necessitate infallibility. And I suggest that the problem of hallucinations, which has preoccupied many philosophers, has often been misconceived. It is, I would hold, quite wrong to talk about hallucinations as phenomenalists do, as if they were due to well-behaved perception of misbehaved objects; they are due to disorder in perception itself. If a drunkard 'sees rats that are not there', as we say, this does not mean that there is a special species of rat, the *rattus inexistens*, which the drunkard has a peculiar capacity for observing, co-ordinate with, but less common than, the more familiar *rattus rattus* and *rattus norvegicus*; it means that there is no such thing as the drunkard's rat, he only 'thinks there is'. Misperceptions are not due to normal awareness of a 'wild' sense-datum; it is the awareness that is wild, otherwise the percipient would not be perceiving the particular sense-datum at all.[1] On the other hand, this does not mean that we have no criteria for distinguishing authentic from hallucinatory perception; in the example given, although we do not examine the drunkard's rats we do examine the drunkard. As Fr Peter Chirico writes:

> Man exists in a world. That existence in juxtaposition with the surrounding world is not something to be explained after one has asserted self-awareness but is the initial condition in which self-awareness comes to be. It is a given that can no more be proved than can one's self-awareness. Man comes to recognize that he is a knower and one who is self-aware only at the very moment that he becomes aware of knowing what is other than himself. . . . Practically speaking, then, he becomes aware of himself as an 'I' only to the degree that he accepts the existence of the 'not-I'.[2]

Furthermore, this recognition that the real world is essentially an *intelligible* world, that is to say a world which is the proper object of apprehension by the intelligence and not a world composed of sense-data or sensibilia, will rescue us from the endemic vice of the Victorian theoretical physicist, the obsession of constructing hypothetical microscopic material mechanisms to explain the behaviour of macroscopic material objects.

> Matter was explained away as consisting of invisible atoms and impalpable ether, though with remarkable inconsistency the atoms and the ether themselves were felt to be unexplained until they could be provided with the fundamental properties of geometrical extension, inertia, elasticity, and the like. Gyroscopes and indiarubber and wax and beer-froth were made of matter, and matter was made of ether. But when we inquired what ether was made of it turned out to be gyroscopes, indiarubber, wax, and beer-froth on an ultra-microscopic scale, or at any rate something with properties very like theirs.[3]

And these ultra-microscopic entities were, of course, functioning in three-dimensional Euclidean space, just like the macroscopic entities which they composed. The most that theories of this type can achieve, beyond explaining *obscurum per obscurius*, is to provide analogues, in terms of mass, extension, and motion, for the more 'occult' physical quantities dealt with by sciences such as optics and electromagnetics. With the arrival of relativity and, still more, of quantum-theory, their collapse became more or less complete, and scientists of the eminence of Eddington and Schroedinger retreated into varieties of Kantian subjectivism. If, however, the world is an intelligible entity, and if intelligibility has a wider range than sensibility, such a retreat is both unnecessary and uncalled-for:

> The world does not lose its claim to reality by ceasing to be imaginable as an infinite uniform Euclidean receptacle, populated by tiny rapidly moving massive lumps drifting uniformly down the stream of time, and only recover that claim by becoming imaginable as a four-dimensional non-Euclidean space-time continuum, in which what used to be thought of as material objects are now seen to be wrinkles or puckers. Just as the essence of perception is not sensing

objects but apprehending them, even if we can apprehend them only through the mediation of sense, so the paradigm of a real world is not its sensible imaginability but its intelligible apprehensibility. . . . If, therefore the universe of modern physics is one in which all attempts to make it intelligible by models of sensory type fail and which requires for its systematization the kind of concepts that are used by quantum physics, this does not in the least imply that it is unreal or subjective. It simply means that the formulae of quantum physics express the kind of intelligibility that it has.[4]

Up to a point the Victorian physicist's ambition was legitimate and useful, and it certainly provides a striking instance of the scholastic tag, *mens convertit se ad phantasmata*. Its error was that it looked upon the model which the mind had constructed out of the sensible phenomena as being the ultimate terminus of perception, the *objectum quod*, instead of an *objectum quo* or *medium quo*, through which and by means of which the genuine *objectum quod*, the real intelligible being, is apprehended. Whether we are considering the sense-data, the theories and models of science, or the pictorial structures worked up by the imagination, the same principle of instrumentality applies. All are *objecta quibus* by means of which, and in divers ways in accordance with their diverse characters, we can deepen our understanding of the intelligible universe which is the ultimate and all-embracing *objectum quod*. One model differs from another in glory; there are also models terrestrial and models celestial. Each of them has its own function, which is to help us to grasp, under some particular aspect, the real and intelligible universe in which *ens et verum convertuntur*, being and intelligibility coincide.

Any attempt today to maintain that the human mind can actually apprehend external reality is sure to meet with the challenge that Kant's 'Copernican revolution' put an end to all that. It is important therefore to recall—or to be informed, for most philosophers seem never to have heard about this—that the challenge was taken up on a heroic scale by the Belgian Jesuit Joseph Maréchal in a gigantic work, *Le point de départ de la métaphysique*, in the nineteen-twenties.[5] He did not dispute the legitimacy of starting where Kant started, with the phenomenal object, but he claimed to reach a very different conclusion from Kant's. Students of Maréchal have disputed whether he rejected Kant's method or whether he accepted it but used it to a different result. Strange as it may seem, by his own assertion, he did both! Thus he wrote:

> When confronting the claims of modern criticism, there are two ways of upholding the rights of traditional intellectual realism: (1) to deny, partially or wholly, the legitimacy of the critical demands; (2) to show that metaphysical realism satisfies these demands, even though they are exaggerated or arbitrary. These two approaches do not exclude each other. We shall use both of them.[6]

Maréchal was in fact confident that, by applying the Kantian or 'transcendental' method, it would be possible to construct what could legitimately be called a transcendental Thomism. His basic conviction was that, if we start from the 'conscious phenomenon' or 'object of thought' as it is initially and unavoidably given and analyse the object with all its constituent conditions, we find in it the objective existence of an absolute. It was at this point, a quite basic one, that Maréchal found the fundamental flaw in Kant. For Kant, this relation to an absolute or unconditioned was a regulative but not a constitutive element in the object known, that is to say the mind could not help affirming it but nevertheless it had no basis in reality. Thus, in Otto Muck's words, for Kant, 'knowledge remains phenomenal', while, in contrast,

> Maréchal with the help of transcendental analysis, tries to show that the relation to the unconditioned is constitutive for the phenomenal object and that knowledge thus reaches the fundamental order of being. This means that the phenomenal object cannot be viewed as phenomenal in the exclusive sense.[7]

Maréchal thus felt obliged to follow Kant to the extent of adopting the 'transcendental method', that is to say the procedure of investigating the conditions under which knowledge is possible *before* venturing to construct a metaphysic; but he has been claimed by his followers as a transcendental *Thomist*. Critics such as M. Etienne Gilson, however, have condemned such a programme as putting the cart before the horse and have insisted that without at least an implicit metaphysic it is impossible to discuss the conditions of knowledge or indeed anything else. Gilson would indeed admit that a realist metaphysic, and indeed a Thomist metaphysic, can be *critical* in the sense of giving rise to a critique of knowledge, but he would maintain that the metaphysic must come first, while more extreme opponents of Kant and all that derives from him would condemn the very notion of a critical realism as a contradiction in terms. Without attempting to settle this dispute, which may be at least partly verbal,[8] it will be well to pass to the impressive contemporary figure of Fr Bernard Lonergan, S.J., whose work derives much of its inspiration from Maréchal but is free from the existentialist idiom in which most of Maréchal's disciples have felt it desirable to clothe their thought.

INTELLIGENCE AND INSIGHT

Lonergan's doctrine was expounded at great length and with a wealth of detailed explanation and application in his massive work *Insight: A Study of Human Understanding*, published in 1957,[1] and was further elaborated in *Method in Theology*, published in 1972.[2] I have discussed them in some detail, and also the writings of other leaders of the transcendentalist Thomist school, in my books *The Openness of Being*[3] and *Nature and Supernature*,[4] to which I may refer the reader for references to others of the many comments to which Lonergan's expositions have given rise. Here I shall restrict myself to the particular topic with which we are now concerned, namely Lonergan's role as a defender and expounder of the intellectual principle.

Lonergan's method is transcendental, in the sense that he bases metaphysics upon epistemology and not vice versa; he discusses knowledge first and only then goes on to discuss being; and he adopts the method of proving positions by showing that the counter-positions are self-contradictory. (This is the only method that is available for justifying absolutely primary propositions, since there are *ex hypothesi* no propositions more primary from which they can be derived.) His work *Insight* is divided into two parts of roughly equal size: the first, entitled 'Insight as Activity', answers the question 'What is happening when we are knowing?'; the second, entitled,

'Insight as Knowledge', answers the question 'What is known when that is happening?'. In *Method In Theology*, between these two questions, which he labels as concerned with cognitional theory and metaphysics respectively, he interposes a third question, 'Why is that knowing?', which he labels as concerned with epistemology. Whether in fact as well as in presentation he holds that one must justify the validity of knowledge before one allows oneself the luxury of knowing is not altogether easy to determine; it is possible to quote him for either answer to this question,[5] and fortunately it need not be settled for our immediate purpose. It is however important to see what he has to say about our knowledge of the world.

The title of the book *Insight* indicates its fundamental thesis; it is that knowing consists in penetrating beneath the immediately apprehended surface of an object into its intelligible *being*. Insight is *in*-sight, *seeing into* the observed object, not just receiving an impact from it or, on the other hand, just noticing a flash, though both of these phenomena may occur. In his earlier work *Verbum: Word and Idea in Aquinas*,[6] Lonergan generally uses the word 'understanding', which, like the Latin words *intelligentia* and *intellectus*, carries the same suggestion, to *read beneath* or *within*. He rejects explicitly what he describes as 'the mistaken supposition that knowing consists in taking a look'.[7] In developing his argument, he traces the operation of the inquiring human mind from one level to another, from common-sense awareness of the world, through the various types of mathematical, scientific, aesthetic, and moral experience, up to the level of metaphysics; and at each level of abstraction there is always left an 'empirical residue' which raises further questions and leads to further heights of inquiry. Like Gilson, Lonergan refuses to remain simply in the order of conceptual thought and insists on the importance of the judgement; further—and this is vital to him as to Gilson— he sees the judgement as not only affirming the unity of concepts but also as asserting existence in concrete reality. He makes repeated use of the double notion of 'intelligent grasp and reasonable affirmation', thus bringing concept and judgement together.[8] And he interprets the principle *Mens quodammodo fit omnia* in a thoroughly dynamic manner, according to which the mind has an unrestricted desire to know which can ultimately be satisfied only by God.

It is outside the scope of the present discussion to consider in detail Lonergan's argued case for the existence of the God of Christian theism; I have discussed it elsewhere.[9] It will, however, be of interest to see how the intellectual principle works out in practice in his dynamic interpretation of it. He repeatedly lays down as guides for its application the four maxims 'Be attentive', 'Be intelligent', 'Be reasonable', 'Be responsible.'[10] These are correlated respectively with the four mental activities of experience, understanding, reflection, and decision. I do not think that commentators have sufficiently remarked (perhaps because Lonergan has not) that these are a refinement and elaboration of the fundamental structural operations of the human soul as it is conceived in Thomist Aristotelianism. Experience corresponds to sensation; understanding and reflection to conception and judgement respectively, both of which are operations of the intellect; and all three are forms of cognition. In contrast, the fourth member is an operation of appetition or volition. In diagrammatic form:

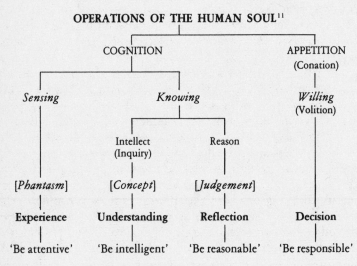

OPERATIONS OF THE HUMAN SOUL[11]

COGNITION   APPETITION (Conation)

Sensing   *Knowing*   *Willing* (Volition)

Intellect (Inquiry)   Reason

[*Phantasm*]   [*Concept*]   [*Judgement*]

Experience   **Understanding**   **Reflection**   **Decision**

'Be attentive'   'Be intelligent'   'Be reasonable'   'Be responsible'

That there is this correspondence is not, I think, surprising, for Lonergan is a Transcendental Thomist, and, whatever the traditional Thomists may say, Transcendental Thomists at any rate believe themselves to be Thomists. The correspondence is, however, not altogether exact and there is a good deal of overlapping and interpenetration, especially when Lonergan applies his scheme to describing and specifying the method of theology. This is fully accounted for by the repudiation of Aristotelian systematics which Lonergan proclaims or, more positively, by the fundamentally dynamic character of his approach.

There are not a few details of Lonergan's system which it is possible to question, and among those who admire his work there are critics as well as disciples; there are also—and this is one of the signs of greatness—those who would describe themselves as both. I have myself indicated some points which are at least in need of clarification.[12] Nevertheless, in his insistence upon the capacity of the human mind to penetrate through the phenomenal level and to achieve insight into the intelligible reality of extra-mental beings he stands out as a most determined defender of the Intellectual Principle. That his demand for a reorientation of Christian thinking in order to meet modern developments in science, philosophy, and hermeneutics does not imply any weakening in this respect is clear from the uncompromising attack upon Dr Leslie Dewart's book *The Future of Belief: Theism in a World Come of Age*[13] which he launched in his article 'The Dehellenization of Dogma'.[14] This is significant in a thinker who, it has been suggested , may have provided the new paradigm which Christian theology urgently needs today and may have reduced the contemporary theological chaos to order in a way parallel to the achievements of Copernicus, Newton, and Lavoisier in the physical sciences.[15]

Most of what I have said until now has been concerned with the capacity possessed by the human mind of apprehending realities other than itself—*mens quodammodo fit omnia*. We must now turn to the other aspect of the Intellectual Principle, that which is concerned with the capacity of the human mind to know the truth, the *adaequatio intellectus ad rem*. Important though this is, we can deal with it more briefly, for it is largely implicit in what has gone before.

The classic definition of truth as conformity between the understanding and the reality which it apprehends—*veritas est adaequatio rei et intellectus*—received widespread acceptance from its endorsement by St Thomas Aquinas,[16] though it goes back far before his time. (M. Maritain points out that St Thomas was mistaken in attributing it to Isaac Israeli (A.D. 845–940) and finds its basis in Aristotle.)[17] It is essential to understand it precisely. We must notice that it asserts a conformity between the *understanding* and the *reality*,[18] not between the *idea* and the reality (as in Cartesianism), nor between the understanding and the *idea* (as in Berkeleian and some later idealism), nor between the understanding and the *name*, nor between the *name* and the reality (as in various types of logical and linguistic empiricism). Both the *idea* (the sensible species, phenomenon, sense-datum, sensibile, sensum) and the *name* (the word or linguistic entity) are extremely important media in the activity of seeking and attaining truth and in communicating truth to other members of the human community; but truth itself consists in the accurate apprehension of reality by an intellect, an understanding, a mind, and to substitute for either of the terms of this concrete intercourse either one of the media, or some element of one of the media, or a logical construct formed out of such elements, even if such a construct has the same logical properties and relations as the authentic term which it has supplanted, is to eviscerate the act of knowing of its vital and dynamic character and to substitute an unearthly ballet of bloodless categories in its place. (To say this is not to deny the legitimacy of either logical or linguistic studies as such, but only to protest at their usurpation of the place that belongs to a metaphysically based doctrine of knowledge and of truth.) When, therefore, we assert that truth consists in the conformity of the understanding with reality, we are not stating a doctrine about the use of language, although we are using language in order to make a statement and although, at a higher level of abstraction, we may state a doctrine about the use of language later on (as in fact we are doing *inter alia* at this moment); when we assert that truth consists in the conformity of the understanding with reality, we are making a statement, by implication, about the capacity of the understanding, the mind, to become, 'intentionally', beings other than itself. Formally, we may be simply giving a definition of truth, decreeing the connotation which the word 'truth' is to have; but, since we are hardly likely to define an entity which we believe to be impossible of occurrence, we are tacitly implying that the conformity, the *adaequatio*, between *intellectus* and *res* is at least possible. Conformity, *adaequatio*, can, of course, be of various kinds, and its precise character will depend on the terms which it relates; in the present case they are a mind which is intelligent and a reality which is intelligible. And, since it is of the very essence of mindhood that a mind can 'intentionally' become anything, it follows that, while the mind and its object are really distinct in the entitative order, they become identical in the order of knowledge. *Intellectus in actu est intellectum in actu.* [19] There is little use in trying to elucidate the special character of this 'conformity' by seeking something simpler, more primitive, or more familiar with which to compare it; for there is nothing simpler or more primitive, and it is already entirely familiar to us. The most that can or need be done to justify it is to show either that the counter-positions suffer from internal self-contradiction or else that, whenever they try to defend themselves, they have to invoke the aid of the position which they formally reject.

This being so, we can, I think, now see how wrong-headed was the attempt of the logical positivists of the nineteen-twenties to lay down criteria for the meaningfulness of linguistic statements, not merely in the sense that they failed to find criteria that were satisfactory but in the more serious sense that the quest could not even be meaningfully announced without assuming that it had already been solved. It is, of course, now well known that the pristine simplicity of the original Verification Principle, with its bland proclamation that a sentence was meaningful only if the proposition which it expressed was either logically tautologous or empirically verifiable, was marred by the drawback that the Principle so defined ruled out itself as meaningless; while the various mitigations of the Principle which were proposed in order to eliminate its suicidal character had a far less obvious appearance and looked suspiciously as if they had been devised deliberately to discriminate between different classes of sentences in accordance with the specifications and requirements of their authors. [20] But the basic error of the logical positivists, as of many of their successors, was the assumption that some extrinsic criterion of meaningfulness is necessary. In the last resort, the only way to discover whether a statement is meaningful is to see whether it conveys meaning; the only way to test it for intelligibility is to see whether it can be understood. The apparently vacuous and tautologous character of these last assertions is in fact their strength; for it arises from the fact that words do not cruise about under their own steam in a kind of linguistic paradise, each generating its own meaning or bearing it as a kind of semantic birthright.[21] They are instruments devised and utilized, largely but not entirely unconsciously, by intelligent beings in their intercourse with one another and with other beings as well. It is of course true that modern linguistic philosophers have abandoned the crudities of their logical positivist predecessors and have discussed at great length the linguistic habits of other human beings, but they have made this a primarily behavioural study, a study of the conditions under which certain types of human beings emit certain types of linguistic utterances, and have tended to identify the meanings of sentences with the conditions of their pronouncement. Very rarely and as little as possible do they seek for the meanings within the mental life of the utterers, and still less do they show interest in this mental life when no utterances are being made. The chief exception—and it is an ominous and revealing one—is concerned with the utterances which they make, whether orally or in writing, when expounding their own views; very few, if any, are willing to identify the meaning of their own theories with the conditions under which they have been stimulated to give them verbal expression. Their own theorizing, if no one else's, is an *adaequatio intellectus ad rem*. Constantly, when reading the modern linguistic philosophers, one is led to wonder what would happen if they examined their own writings in the light of their own theories and to feel surprise that they do not venture on the experiment. From the later writings of Ludwig Wittgenstein in particular one derives the impression of a man who was obsessed and almost tortured by the sense that all human attempts at philosophizing turn out to be nothing but more or less systematic manipulation of words, but who never faced the consequences of the fact that his own expositions and explorations were conducted in the same linguistic medium.

MIND AND REALITY

It is, I suggest, time that we frankly admitted that thinking and knowing are activities of the human intelligence, and that truth consists in the conformity of the mind with reality and not in a schematic or logical correlation of words with phenomena. In this life of the intelligence, words, concepts, and images all play their several parts, but as instruments and not as termini of the acts of understanding and perception. So does the elaborate physical, physiological, and psychological mechanism that is involved in sensory perception. All these are *objecta* or *media quibus*, not *objecta quae*, of perception, means by which, not objects which, we perceive. (They may, of course, become *objecta quae* in later acts; an oculist may examine my retina, which is then an *objectum quod*, but his own retina is an *objectum quo* while he does this.) And, because truth consists in the conformity of the *mind* with its real object, the *res*, and not in the labelling of the object with a name, we must look for the meaningfulness and the meaning of language in its use by intelligent human beings. In order to see whether a sentence is meaningful you should not ask whether or not it conforms to some extrinsic criterion but whether it is used with a meaning in some community of intelligent people. Language is indeed extremely important; as Julian Huxley remarked, one of the things that distinguishes man from the lower animals is 'the invention of words as symbols for things, in place of sounds as signs for feelings'.[1] But it is important precisely *because* words are symbols; and words are symbols because human beings, who have intelligent minds, give them *meanings*, either explicitly by designation or implicitly by using them meaningfully. Words do not grow on trees with labels attached to each indicating its meaning. Truth, as the classic definition affirmed, is found when there is conformity between the understanding and reality, not between *language* and reality, and it is in the understanding that meaning is to be found. It is only in a secondary and derivative sense that truth and meaning are to be found in the linguistic realm. As I have written elsewhere:

> While we have only our own human languages in which to assert truths, the truths themselves are something other than our assertions of them and are not in themselves linguistic at all. That is to say, a statement is true to the extent that, in the social and linguistic context in which it is uttered, it accurately describes some features of the real or the logical world, and it can perform this function even if it can never reproduce with complete adequacy the feature's total complexity. Language has inevitably a certain looseness of fit at both the objective and the subjective poles.[2]

And again, with the later abandoned ideals of the earlier Wittgenstein in mind:

> So far from consisting of atomic facts which can be put in one-to-one correspondence with atomic linguistic statements, the world (at least as it appears to us) is a continuous, multidimensional, dynamic entity, while language is discrete, one-dimensional and static. And even if we interpret current physical theory as showing that the universe consists of discrete 'fundamental particles', probably finite in number, so that its ostensible continuity is only an appearance, it will still be of such vast complexity that it cannot possibly be pictured biuniquely by any set of statements that we could ever manage to formulate.
>
> What I am in fact arguing is that it is a mistake to suppose that the function of language is, even ideally, to picture reality by being in biunique correspondence with it, except in certain limited and highly specialized cases. Its function is rather to be an instrument by which intelligent beings are able both to clarify their own thinking and to communicate their thoughts to one another.[3]

And again:

> We must in fact avoid two opposite extremes. One is that of assuming that the ideal to which language should strive is simply that of picturing facts by statements logically isomorphous with them; this was the view of the earlier Wittgenstein. For it, an ideal language would be one in which every object and relation had been given a label and all the thinking could be done by a computer. The other extreme is that of minimizing the function of language as expressing and communicating truth, or of redefining truth so that it no longer consists of the conformity of thought with reality but of an ever-changing vocalization of man's subjective experience as a changing inhabitant of a changing world. This is the view defended by Dr Dewart with his repeated denunciations of 'Hellenism'.[4]

Once we have recognized that truth is concerned with insight into reality and not with the assignment of verbal labels we shall be in a position to approach the question, much canvassed today, of pluralism in theology. It is, of course, possible for the notion of pluralism to be abused and to be handled un-scrupulously; it is difficult not to suspect that some Roman Catholic members of the radical *avant garde* have appealed to it, not because they really wished to see a plurality of theological attitudes but because they wished that one par-ticular brand of theological monopoly should be eliminated simply in order that its place should be taken by another. Nevertheless, as soon as it is recognized that the way in which men think and speak inevitably bears the marks of the social and cultural setting of time and place in which they live, the question demands to be considered of the relation between the unchanging gospel and the constantly changing forms under which Christian thinkers have discussed and expounded it. Pope John's famous assertion that 'the substance of the ancient doctrine of the deposit of faith is one thing, and the way in which it is presented is another'[5] states the problem succinctly but does not as it stands do anything to solve it. Theologians of the eminence of Fr Karl Rahner[6] and Fr Bernard Lonergan[7] have given their attention to it. In Fr Peter Chirico's exhaustive and stimulating work *Infallibility: the Crossroads of Doctrine*,[8] the theme of pluralism is constantly present and, although some of his conclusions might call for reconsideration, he carries the investigation farther than any other writer with whom I am acquainted. We are not concerned here with his development of the special topic of his book, but I would draw attention to the governing principle by which it is directed. This is the notion of *meaning* as capable of persisting through the various modes and media in which it is expressed. New meanings may emerge, but the basic universal meanings (and these are rooted in the Resurrection of Jesus) do not change, and they are the ground of the Church's infallibility. Admittedly, 'a new situation exists in the Church. We have a pluralism of both meaning and ex-pression to a degree that the past never knew.'[9] This creates problems but it gives no excuse for despair:

Pluralism is inevitable in the present condition precisely because particular meanings always precede universal meanings, sometimes by centuries. Yet pluralism must not be viewed as an end in itself; rather, it is a stage towards the richness of eschatological unity. This means that all meanings or actualizations of human potential are ultimately shareable and hence universal, but not now. Pluralism has become a problem of greater magnitude in our time because of the rapid and diverse development of particular sectors of meaning without a corresponding development of the capacity to unify.[10]

Thus Chirico is very different from the kind of pluralist who thinks it is desirable to have as many theologies as possible, each developing on its own lines and none having any particular relation to any others. He does not advocate the permanent co-existence of a mass of mutually inconsistent systems on the ground that none of them can ever be shown to be true anyhow. But he does not, on the other hand, wish to see any one system prematurely and monopolistically elbowing out all the others and refusing to learn from any of them. Pluralism is, for him, an essentially transient and fluid condition, relative to the Church's pilgrim situation as *in via* and not yet *in patria*. And behind this there lies the conviction which I stressed earlier in this discussion, that *meaning* can be the same under a variety of linguistic and conceptual vehicles. And this is so because truth consists in the conformity of the intelligence to reality and not just to language or concepts. Reality itself is therefore intelligible, thát is to say *meaningful*. It was with this in mind that the scholastics were able, while predicating truth primarily of the relation between the intellect and its object, to predicate it, analogously and derivatively, of any being that was real and not fictitious, simply in virtue of its status as a potential object for an intellect, and to declare *Omne ens est verum*.

It will be well, as this discussion comes to a close, to make it plain that, in defending the classical thesis that truth consists in the conformity of the intelligence to reality, I have no intention of reducing religion to a bare intellectual assent to propositions. The essence of religion is the love of God and our neighbour, and behind any love that we can exercise there is the primordial fact that God first loved us. Nevertheless, in the very act of affirming this we are making a judgement about reality. No one, however 'anti-intellectualistic' his attitude may be, can afford to dispense with the Intellectual Principle, unless he has reached the extreme detachment of indifference to his own attitude. If he tells us, with Dr Leslie Dewart, that 'truth is not the adequacy of our representative operations, but the adequacy of our conscious existence',[11] he must not be surprised if we ask him whether he considers that the representative operation which he has just performed is adequate or not, and whether, if he considers that it is adequate, he is not implying that it is 'true'. If, with Mr Clifford Longley, he makes the sweeping assertion that 'the main theological controversies, of the past or the present, have not been about an academic abstraction called Truth but about the deep and potent influence that religious myth can have on the slow long-term evolution of social values,'[12] he must expect some awkward traditionalist to point out that, whatever may be the case with theological controversies, he has himself just made use of this 'academic abstraction' in the mere fact of making an assertion. For there is really nothing academic, in the pejorative sense, about the notion of Truth at all. It lies at the base of all sane human intercourse, civilized and uncivilized alike. It is what children are taught to tell and what even liars hope they will be thought to be telling. It is what every witness in a court of law is placed under oath to respect and for disregard of which he may be sentenced for perjury. The capacity to recognize it differentiates man from the brutes. It is the ground of what I have described as the Intellectual Principle. And that, as I said at the beginning, is so obvious that hardly anyone but philosophers and theologians would think of questioning it.

2 *On from Chalcedon*

The Christian formula is not: 'Humanity manifests certain
adumbrations of the divine', but: 'This man was very God.'

Dorothy L. Sayers

IS CHALCEDON RELEVANT TODAY?

In A.D. 451 the Council of Chalcedon, commonly reckoned as
the Fourth Ecumenical, expressed the Church's faith in the
incarnation in the following words, which, except in those
churches generally known as either Nestorian on the one hand
or monophysite on the other, have come to be accepted as the
classical definition of orthodox Christian belief:

> Following, therefore, the holy fathers, we all unanimously
> teach that men should acknowledge one and the same Son,
> our Lord Jesus Christ, the same perfect in Godhead and the
> same perfect in manhood, truly God and truly man, the
> same of a rational soul and body, consubstantial
> (*homoousios*) with the Father in Godhead and the same
> consubstantial with us in manhood, like us in all things
> except sin; begotten of the Father before the ages as regards
> his Godhead, and the same, in the last days, for us and for
> our salvation, begotten of Mary the Virgin, the Mother of
> God (*theotokos*), as regards his manhood; one and the same
> Christ, Son, Lord, only-begotten, made known in two
> natures (*en duo phusesin*), without confusion, without
> change, without division, without separation, the difference
> of the natures being in no way removed by the union, but
> the property of each nature being preserved and coming
> together into one person (*prosopon*) and subsistence
> (*hypostasis*), not parted or divided into two persons, but one
> and the same Son, only-begotten, God, Word, Lord Jesus
> Christ, as the prophets of old and Jesus Christ himself have
> taught us about him and the creed of the Fathers has handed
> down to us.

It will be my purpose to argue here that the Definition of

Chalcedon is the truth and nothing but the truth, but also that it is not the whole truth. And first it will be necessary to consider certain objections to the Definition which are frequently voiced today.

(1) The first objection is that the Definition emerged from, and is expressed in the concepts and terms of, a fifth-century Greek philosophical system which is discredited among modern philosophers and is in addition alien to the minds of modern men and women whether they are philosophers or not. It must be said in reply that in the Definition no particular *philosophical* doctrines are adopted or even assumed, except that of personal identity; an extreme Humean might find himself rebuffed but hardly anyone else. The doctrines expressed are all *theological*. Admittedly, certain words are used which were also used by philosophers, but they were also words with usage in common speech: 'being' (*ousia*), 'nature' (*physis*), 'person' (*prosopon* and *hypostasis*). And, so far from Christian thinking being forced into the conceptual and verbal moulds of Greek philosophy, it is striking that when Christian thinkers did experiment with Greek words and concepts they found themselves obliged to impose modifications and distinctions that philosophy had hitherto not known, such as the distinction between *ousia* and *hypostasis*. The technical uses that such terms come to have in Christian theology come not from philosophy but from Christianity.[1] In any case, the Chalcedonian Definition is remarkably free from technicalities. It is somewhat repetitive, for the sake of emphasis and in order to exclude specific errors; but its positive assertion is simple in the extreme. It is that the Lord Jesus Christ is one person, and that he is truly and perfectly God and is truly and perfectly man. It is not denied that this is a great and wonderful mystery or that it raises deep and perhaps insoluble problems for the human mind; but the statement itself is brief and lucid.

(2) Then it is objected that the Definition is formal (in the modern sense of 'formal') and static. This must be allowed, but it must be remembered that the Definition does not claim to give an exhaustive theological account of the incarnation. Like the Council itself, it was a response to certain false views about the *constitution* of Christ, such as that he had no human soul, that the subject of his human life was not the Eternal Son, that his human nature had no distinct reality, and so on. It therefore

29

stressed the *product* of the incarnation, if the term may be allowed, rather than the *process* or the *purpose*. And, like other necessary rebuttals of heresy it may have led to a certain temporary one-sidedness, though it must not be forgotten that the Definition is only part, though the culminating and focal part, of the whole Decree of the Council of Chalcedon. The Decree explicitly endorses, and quotes in full, the Creeds of Nicaea and Constantinople,[2] and these are anything but static: '. . . who because of us men and because of our salvation *came down from heaven and was incarnate* . . .'. And behind all this there lies the thoroughly dynamic Christology of fathers such as Irenaeus and Athanasius.

(3) Thirdly, there is the view of Chalcedon summed up in the much-quoted assertion of William Temple that 'the formula of Chalcedon [by which he meant the formula "one person, two natures"] is in fact a confession of the bankruptcy of Greek Patristic Theology.'[3] Years later, Temple amplified his epigram by saying: 'It is really not the formula, but the history of the whole controversy, that leaves the impression of bankruptcy. The formula did exactly what an authoritative formula ought to do: it stated the fact.'[4] And even in his original essay he had added that the formula 'preserved belief in our Lord's real humanity',[5] an important characteristic that not all critics of Chalcedon have recognized. Nevertheless, the notion that Christology came to a full stop with Chalcedon has become deeply rooted in English-speaking theological circles, though value-judgements on it vary from the 'high-church' view that with Chalcedon Christology reached its triumphant climax, after which it did nothing more because there was nothing more for it to do, to the 'low-church' view that, in yielding to the seductions of non-scriptural and Greek modes of thought, Christology had from the start been engaged on a perverse and non-Christian course, which by the time of Chalcedon had led it to the end of a blind alley where it died of sheer frustration and inanition. But to virtually nobody did the suspicion occur that, in spite of its climactic character, Chalcedon had not brought Greek Christology to either a glorious or a miserable demise.

The reasons for this attitude to Chalcedon are not easy to find; it is on the whole an Anglo-Saxon phenomenon and is not paralleled on the European continent. It coheres with the common tendency in Anglicanism to give a peculiarly authoritative doctrinal status to the first four General Councils, a tendency that receives statutory support from the Act of Parliament 1 Eliz. I cap. 1 and the personal backing of the weighty names of Hooker and Andrewes.[6] It has been vastly encouraged in practice—though it is difficult here to see precisely what is cause and what is effect—by the fact that syllabuses on the History of Early Christian Doctrine have almost invariably set their *terminus ad quem* at A.D. 451 and writers have followed suit. The widely used *Introduction to the Early History of Christian Doctrine to the Time of the Council of Chalcedon*[7] by J. F. Bethune-Baker, which for nearly half a century after its publication in 1903 moulded the outlook of Anglican ordinands, was explicit about its horizon. Dr J. N. D. Kelly's erudite work *Early Christian Doctrines*,[8] which proposed itself for the succession, maintains the same limits, as does Dr M. F. Wiles's *Christian Fathers*[9] and, with a somewhat different purpose in view, his *Making of Christian Doctrine*.[10] Now it may well be true that, if doctrinal studies are to occupy the small amount of time that the syllabuses allow them and if in addition, for motives of safety or whatever, they have to be considered historically rather than systematically, the middle of the fifth century is as far as the struggling student's burdened mind can be expected to get. I do not think, however, that this is the whole explanation. If it were, I should expect to see far more advanced study and research being done in post-, as contrasted with pre-Chalcedonian, Christology than in fact takes place, and I should expect a very different attitude to the achievements and the significance of Chalcedon from that which we actually find in the English manuals. British writers appear to be firmly committed to what I would label as the 'Syllabus Error'—the view that Christology came to a dead end in A.D. 451 and only revived in the nineteenth century with Schleiermacher; one of the few exceptions is provided by R. V. Sellers's *Council of Chalcedon*,[11] published in 1953. Continental theologians know much better, as can be seen from the writings of Claude Tresmontant,[12] Louis Bouyer,[13] and Walter Kasper.[14] Only recently have two relevant works appeared in English, and both of them in the United States: *Christ in Eastern Christian Thought*[15] by John Meyendorff, and *The Spirit of Eastern Christendom (600–1700)*,[16] which is the second volume of Jaroslav Pelikan's five-volume work *The Christian Tradition*. For all these writers, Chalcedon needed for its clarification and precision that subsequent period of vigorous, and indeed violent, controversy whose climax came with the Fifth Ecumenical Council in 553 and did not really find a point of relative stability until the Seventh in 787. This is far from reducing Chalcedon to a merely episodic status, but it rescues it from irrelevance as a *cul-de-sac*. In Meyendorff's words, 'The Council of Chalcedon . . . opened a new era in the history of Eastern Christian thought.[17] And I shall suggest that that era is not yet closed.

I have said that Chalcedon needed clarification and precision, and this is specially true about one phrase in the Definition, that in which the property of each nature is spoken of as coalescing or 'coming together' into one person (one *prosopon* and one *hypostasis*). The question is whether the one person exists before the two natures come together into it (as, for example, a room in which two people meet exists before they come into it) or whether the person is brought into existence by the coming together of the two natures (as when a molecule of water comes into existence by the coming together of atoms of hydrogen and oxygen). There is, it must be observed, no doubt about the pre-existence of the 'one Christ, Son, Lord, only-begotten', who is the subject of the two natures, for one of the natures is divine, and in that divine nature he was 'begotten from the Father before the ages'; and if confirmation of this is needed it is provided by the Council's endorsement of the Nicene and Constantinopolitan creeds. What is not stated explicitly is that this common *subject* of the two natures is to be described as a *person* before the union of the natures has taken place. Whether the omission of such a statement is a sheer oversight or a subtle concession to the school of Antioch may be a matter of dispute; the matter might seem to be purely verbal but for the controversy that occupied the century after Chalcedon. Was there a real difference of meaning between the view of a composite hypostasis in Christ, as held by Leontius of Byzantium, and the view of the pre-existent Logos as Christ's hypostasis, as held by Leontius of Jerusalem?[18] In any case, the ambiguity was cleared up by the Fifth Ecumenical Council, Constantinople II, in A.D. 553; the person, the *prosopon* or *hypostasis*, of Christ is the pre-existent Son and Word of the

Father. To describe this view, with J. Lebon and others, as neo-Chalcedonian rather than as Chalcedonian perhaps manifests excessive caution. Even if we suppose that, by the terms *prosopon* and *hypostasis*, Chalcedon intended to denote the *complex* formed by the two natures and not their *subject*—though, for the reasons I have given, I think this very unlikely—it will still be clear, from the Definition as a whole and its context in the Decree, that Chalcedon held that the *subject* of each of the two natures was none other than the eternal and pre-existent Son.

JESUS HUMAN AND DIVINE

What, let us now inquire, is the relevance of Chalcedon to Christian belief today? What, if any, are the strong points that should make it of interest to us from more than a purely historical and antiquarian standpoint? First, I would suggest, its insistence upon the reality and completeness of Jesus' humanity. Orthodox Christians in the world of today have had to devote so much effort to defending the divinity of Christ against attacks from within as well as from outside the Christian community, that both they and their opponents have sometimes forgotten that traditional Christology, with its roots in Chalcedon, is committed no less strongly to defending, in its concrete fullness, his humanity. And it has been very largely left to the proponents of the various 'New Christologies' to perform, in their own ways, this necessary task. Nevertheless, nothing could be clearer than Chalcedon's affirmation that Jesus is 'truly man, the same of a rational soul and body', with its deliberate exclusion of the Apollinarian view that in Jesus the person of the divine Word took the place of a rational soul; and further emphasis was added by the Council of 680 (Constantinople III) with its insistence that the rational soul included a human will. Nothing, it was implied, needed to be absent from Christ's human nature to make room for the divine Word, for the Word was not *part* of the human nature but its metaphysical *subject*; *person* and *nature* are not on the same level of being.

But, secondly, complete and concrete though the human nature is, its subject, its person, is literally divine. It is *God* who was born at Bethlehem, who walked and taught in Galilee, who died on the cross and who rose on Easter Day, and not somebody else, a different individual named Jesus. It is noteworthy that the Antiochenes prided themselves on the fact that, by making the man Jesus and not the eternal Word the subject of the suffering and death, they preserved the impassibility of God. (It is ironical that most of their modern sympathizers have no concern with the impassibility of God and that many of them are adherents of process-theology and see God and the world as together involved in change and mutual development.) Now Chalcedon is in fact emphatic on the impassibility of the Godhead: 'it expels from the company of the priests those who dare to say that the Godhead of the Only-begotten is passible'. But, by providing the eternal Word with a complete and concrete human nature which is subject to suffering, it makes it possible for the eternal Word, who is absolutely impassible in his Godhead, to be really and literally passible in his manhood; any element of docetism is altogether ruled out from the passion. Chalcedon was not trying to write metaphysics but simply to preserve the truth of the Christian Gospel, and the formula 'one person, two natures' requires no philosophical expertise for its understanding. Nevertheless by implication it made a metaphysical distinction of great importance which had never been clearly made before. In Meyendorff's words:

> The hypostasis is not the product of nature: it is that in which nature exists, the very principle of its existence. Such a conception of hypostasis can be applied to Christology, since it implies the possibility of a fully human existence, without any limitation, 'enhypostatized' in the Word, who is a divine hypostasis. This conception assumes that God, as personal being, is not totally bound to his own nature; the hypostatic existence is flexible, 'open'; it admits the possibility of divine acts outside of the nature (energies) and implies that God can personally and freely assume a fully human existence while remaining God, whose nature remains completely transcendent.[1]

And again, with reference to one of the leading interpreters of Chalcedon:

> In the explanation Leontius of Jerusalem gave the formula 'one of the Holy Trinity suffered in the flesh', he established the absolute distinction between hypostasis and nature, a

distinction that neither Cyril nor the Antiochene theologians
had fully accepted. In his explanation the Word remains
impassible in his divine nature but suffers in his human
nature. Since, from the moment of the incarnation, the
human nature had become as fully *his own* as the divine
nature, one may (and one must) say that the 'Word suffered'
hypostatically, in his own flesh, because his hypostasis is not
a mere product of the divine nature but is an entity ontologically distinct from the nature, the ego that 'possesses'
the divine nature and 'assumes' the human nature in order to
die and to rise again.[2]

Thus it is, I would maintain, the great strength of Chalcedon
that it meets the two demands which, we are repeatedly told,
are made by the modern mind upon Christologists, but which
the 'New Christologies' seem quite incapable of satisfying
together, namely, first the attribution to Jesus of a complete
and fully concrete human nature, and secondly an intimate,
and not just a remote, involvement of God in the events of the
passion and death of Christ. The alternatives to Chalcedon
which we are offered give us either an undeniably human Jesus,
a 'man for others' or even 'man for God', but a man whose
relation to God is not qualitatively different from that of any
other holy man in history, or else, as in the 'kenotic theories',
they make God the subject of Jesus' life, but only at the expense
of substituting a mutilated or scaled-down divine nature for the
genuinely human nature of the Jesus of the Gospels. There is
indeed mystery at the heart of the Chalcedonian doctrine, as
there is at the heart of the Gospels, but mystery is not absurdity.
And everything depends upon the fact which neither Christian
thinking nor Christian devotion have found it easy to cling on
to, that person, hypostasis, is not a *part* of nature, not even a
tiny and indetectible part, but is its *subject*. Put in those terms,
this seems abstract and technical, and unreasonable to inflict on
the simple believer; but it is in fact only what he is declaring by
implication every time that he professes his belief in the only-
begotten Son of God, begotten of his Father before all worlds,
who was incarnate by the Holy Ghost of the Virgin Mary and
was made man. And this carries with it an uncompromising and unqualified consequence, that there is no ultimate
metaphysical *incompatibility* between God and manhood,

between the Creator and his creation. If the eternal and un-created Second Person of the Holy Trinity, Very God from Very God, can become the subject of a created nature, conferring upon that nature, in the very act of creating and assuming it, both concrete existence and individual identity, then human nature must have a fundamental *openness* to God. If, in the words of *Quicunque vult*, the incarnation took place 'not by the conversion of Godhead into flesh but by the taking up of manhood into God', if, that is, manhood is *assumed* , it must be *assumable*; *ab esse ad posse valet consecutio*. This is, of course, a dignity that manhood cannot achieve by its own efforts, it depends for its actualization upon the love and power of God; but God, in bringing it about, is not doing violence to the inherent structure and functioning of human nature but rather bringing them to a fulfilment which they cannot procure for themselves.[3] Still less (if the phrase makes sense in the context) is he overriding a logical impossibility. And all this, we must observe, is true, not because there is no qualitative difference between God and his creation, but because of the precise way in which they are ultimately and metaphysically diverse. For the contrast between divine and created being is that between being that is altogether self-existent and being that is altogether dependent on self-existent being. The orientation of created being towards God and its openness to him is the basic ontological fact about it. That this openness includes a fitness for assumption into hypostatic union we could perhaps never have suspected, and still less that that assumption had taken place; but when it has occurred we can see how appropriate it is. What I find quite astonishing is the tendency among our modern liberal theologians to deny the incarnation in any but a purely metaphorical sense under the impression that by doing this they are safeguarding the genuine humanity of Jesus. Thus the highly respected American scholar Dr John Knox not only declares that 'We can have the humanity [of Jesus] without the pre-existence and we can have the pre-existence without the humanity. There is absolutely no way of having both',[4] but also asserts that 'it is impossible, *by definition*, that God should become a man',[5] taking the philosophically dubious short cut of drawing conclusions about fact from premises of logic. Dr M. F. Wiles dislikes an incarnational Christology on the grounds that it ascribes to Jesus a type of uniqueness which is difficult to reconcile with the kind of deism which he hopes will be acceptable to the modern world, one which holds that God never acts in any particular events and persons in ways substantially different from those in which he acts in all events and persons.[6] Mr Don Cupitt rightly observes that 'The assertion that deity itself and humanity are permanently united in the one person of the incarnate Lord suggests an ultimate synthesis, a conjunction and continuity between things divine and things of this world. As the popular maxim had it, Grace does not destroy but perfects Nature.' But he goes on to denounce what he openly describes as 'the Christ of Christendom' on the alleged ground that 'Christianity's proper subtlety and freedom depended upon Jesus' ironical perception of *disjunction* between the things of God and the things of men', whereas 'the doctrine of the incarnation unified things which Jesus had kept in ironic contrast with each other.'[7] In consequence, not only the leading Christian thinkers down the ages, Catholic, Orthodox, and Protestant, stand condemned together in his eyes, but so does the tradition of Christian art, and the only real Christian heroes appear to be the Iconoclasts. One thing at least is clear, that belief about Christ and about creation can be very closely connected.

I said at the start of this discussion that I believed that the Definition of Chalcedon was the truth and nothing but the truth, but not that it was the whole truth. And I believe that it both needs and is patent of much more exploration and extension than it has in fact received. It may well be that the very authority which it has been accorded in Christendom has led to it being treated too often as a static and finished product and to its potentialities for development being ignored. Like a sacred relic, it has been sealed off from contamination, placed in a shrine, and contemplated with deep veneration, but not very much has been done with it. Meyendorff, as we have seen, has pointed out that Chalcedon opened a new era in the history of Eastern Christian thought, but that era hardly extended beyond Constantinople III in A.D. 680 and even its modern supporters have tended to respect it for its past achievement rather than for promise still to be fulfilled. Nobody could doubt the orthodoxy of Fr Robert Butterworth, S.J., but his recent article 'Has Chalcedon a Future?'[8] gives only a very tentative and conditional affirmative answer to the question which it posed. I wish, however, to conclude by pointing to a number of questions which are urgent for theology today, on some of which I believe Chalcedon can throw a good deal of light, on some of which I believe Chalcedon needs supplementing, but on none of which I see any need for withdrawal from Chalcedon's position. 'Back to Chalcedon' is, I think, a slogan of only limited utility; 'On from Chalcedon' should be both fruitful and inspiring, and it is very much overdue. What, then, are some of the problems of which Chalcedon did not treat, but on which it may still have guidance to give us?

THE FIRST-CENTURY JEW THE UNIVERSAL SAVIOUR

First, there is the problem how someone who, from the standpoint of the historian, is simply one among the many Jews who were born in Palestine in the reign of Caesar Augustus can be the saviour of mankind in all ages and all places. How can this *particular* man be the *universal* saviour? On a docetic or a monophysite view of Jesus, according to which his human appearance was a mere phantom, so that the only real substance and energy in him was that of the eternal and divine Son, the problem would hardly arise, for salvation would be only an aspect, or at most an extension, of creation. But if the humanity of Jesus is taken seriously in all its concreteness and completeness—as it was taken by Chalcedon, however much it may have been subsequently underemphasized by many who professed to be adherents of Chalcedon—the fact must be accepted—and not accepted in a regretful or embarrassed manner but vigorously and insistently affirmed—that if the Word was to become man at all he could only become man as a member of one particular people, sharing the physical and mental features of one particular culture, in one particular place, and at one particular time. This is not altered by the fact that the human race as a whole has a genuine unity which transcends all its local, temporal, and ethnic varieties, but it does mean that the phrase 'the scandal of particularity', which was common in some circles between the Wars, is highly misleading. The particularity of Jesus is not a scandal for Chalcedonian Christology; it is of its very essence. We can therefore only welcome the contemporary emphasis upon the genuineness and completeness of Jesus' human nature. And this makes it all the more understandable that writers, such as

Dr Hick and Dr Nineham, who reject the concept of the in-carnation,[1] find it difficult if not impossible to hold that Jesus is the unique saviour of the whole human race. If, however, we accept, with Chalcedon, that the hypostasis, the person, of Jesus is the eternal Word, the universal agent of creation, *per quem omnia facta sunt*, and if, with many of the fathers, we see redemption as the renewal and fulfilment of creation, we shall not be tempted to deprive Christ's humanity of either its concreteness or its particularity in order to allow for his universal relationship and relevance. But this, of course, will depend on our readiness to affirm, in contrast with much modern liberal theology, the genuine compatibility between divinity and humanity. And this leads on to a further point.

In speaking of the 'compatibility' between divinity and humanity in Christ, we are concerned with something more than a merely logical or even metaphysical relation of non-repugnance, though both these are included. We are not to hold that Jesus' human particularity as a first-century Palestinian Jew so insulates him from all other times, places, and cultures that his human nature has no affinity with ours and that his relation to us as the universal redeemer resides solely where it originates, in his divine person. By assuming human nature into union with his person, the divine Word imparted to it not only concrete existence but also his own universality, without depriving it of its own particularity. Indeed, his own universality and its own particularity are communicated to it together by the single act through which it is created and assumed. And, since *ab esse ad posse valet consecutio*, not only must humanity be assumable by God but also particularity must be assumable by universality. And therefore Jesus *as man* is both particular and universal. Paradoxical as it might seem, he is both identified with his concrete historical setting and also radically transcends it; this is precisely the picture which the Gospels give of him, baffling as it is to the liberal Christologists.

A brief digression may be desirable here. In speaking as I have just done, I may appear to be committing Christian faith to the Aristotelian theory (whatever that may be, for it is not easy to determine) of particulars and universals. Is Chalcedon, after all, more subtly than first appeared, tied up with con-temporary Greek philosophy? I do not think so. That there is a mysterious interconnection between particulars and universals is a pre-philosophical datum, a fact of life, of which every philosophical system has to attempt an account; this is true even of medieval nominalism and modern linguistic empiricism. (Somewhat similarly, the doctrine of analogy is not an attempt to make it possible to speak about God, but to explain how such an extraordinary activity has been possible.) It was Christian belief—the belief that Jesus is God incarnate and is the redeemer of all mankind—and not Aristotelian or any other type of fifth-century philosophy that led Christian thinkers to see that, whatever might be the case in other natural species, in man there is a profound and highly mysterious relation between the universal and the particular, which it was essential to maintain even if no existing philosophical system could give an adequate account of it. (We might find a modern parallel, in the secular sphere, in the human-rights movements. Many people passionately maintain that there are certain fundamental rights which pertain to all human beings as such, in contrast to sub-human species, simply because they are members of the human race apart from any religious considerations, although neither the philosophical empiricism nor the biological evolutionism which these people profess implies any status of metaphysical uniqueness for man.) I am in fact inclined to hold that, to use the Aristotelian terminology, the relation between the particular individual and the universal species is always an analogical one, ranging at one extreme from the fundamental particles of physics, for which the relation borders on univocity with the type being all-important while individuality has only a numerical significance and hardly that, to the other extreme of manhood, where the individual becomes of supreme importance and his individual characteristics are as significant as those that he has in common with others.[2] This speculation need not be followed up here; it is, however, important to recognize that, while it is right to stress the particularity of Jesus' human nature, as regards time, place, and cultural context, it would be quite unrealistic to take this as implying that we are entirely unable to share his outlook or to understand his teaching. The welcome modern stress on particularity ought not to lead us to forget that man combines in himself particularity and universality in a mysterious but nevertheless undeniable union; and, even on the natural level, scholars are not entirely unsuccessful in studying and interpreting the outlook and mental functioning of human cultures vastly different from their own, subject though their theories are to the possibility of error and insensitivity. The Christian theologian can go further than this, with the universality that human nature has in Christ.

Lionel Thornton published in 1950, under the title *Revelation and the Modern World*, the first part of his trilogy *The Form of the Servant*.[3] His topic was successively narrowed down; Book I was entitled 'Revelation and Culture' and its first chapter 'Revelation in its Human Setting'. He began by positing the question 'What is the relation between revealed religion and its cultural environment?', and he noted that two possible answers could be, and indeed had been, given: (1) that revelation transcends the environment, (2) that revelation is the product of the environment. Both of these he judged to be inadequate. His own answer was that 'revelation *masters* its environment because God identifies himself with human history in order to transform it', and he saw this principle as given scriptural warrant in the form of the Servant, prefigured in Jacob's wrestling in Genesis 32 and given Christian fulfilment in Philippians 2.7; hence the title of his trilogy.[4] Thornton's work never received the attention that it deserved, partly because it was in advance of the theological climate of his time and partly because of peculiarities of its presentation and difficulties of its style; a serious re-examination of it today would be both illuminating and fruitful. Here I wish only to stress the relevance of his own answer to the Christological field. The principle that divine revelation, and in particular the supreme revelation of the taking up of manhood into God by its union with the person of the divine and eternal Word in Christ, *masters its environment by entering into it*, is manifested both by the combination of particularity and universality in Jesus himself and also by the general capacity of human thought and language to express, truthfully though inadequately, in different particular cultural contexts the universal significance and relevance of the Word made flesh.

THE CONDITIONS OF JESUS' MANHOOD

With these considerations in mind we can pass on to the

41

question which for many modern writers appears to exhaust almost the whole domain of Christology, namely that of the limitations of Jesus' human knowledge. The problem is not merely that of recognizing that Jesus appears to have held beliefs which to many modern people appear to be false, such as that David was the author of Psalm 110 and that certain persons are afflicted with evil spirits. It is much wider and deeper than this. The problem is whether Jesus' particularization and localization as a first-century Jew, deriving his education and mental formation from a highly specialized and restricted environment, are compatible with the status which orthodox Christianity holds him to possess as the teacher of universally relevant truth and the author of universally available salvation. And, put in this way, it is seen to be simply one aspect of the principle which we have seen to be central in Christology, that of the union in Christ of the universal and the particular. And this union is not a merely logical or schematic concept; it is a concrete reality worked out in the blood and sweat of human history, from the protevangelium of Genesis 3.15, through the call of Abraham and the covenant with Moses and the whole prophetic tradition of Israel, to its culmination in Mary, the Virgin Daughter of Sion, in whom particularity has reached its peak where it can be seized hold of by the universality of the Creator himself, so that she becomes in truth *Theotokos*, God's own mother; and, in him who is born from her, particularity and universality are one. Jesus is indeed a first-century Jew, but to be the first-century Jew who Jesus is is to have a consciousness not dominated by the one-sided prejudices, uncriticized presuppositions and ethnic ambitions of first-century Judaism but one in which there has been brought to a focus and a climax the mastering by God of the environment of human history into which he has entered in the whole great adventure of divine revelation and human redemption. We can perhaps now understand that it is not impossible for the mind of a first-century Palestinian Jew, with all the educational and cultural limitations imposed by its particular setting, to be an adequate medium in which its subject could consciously recognize his unique filial relation to the heavenly Father and his own messianic vocation, and could communicate that recognition to his human contemporaries.[1] Indeed we may hazard the suggestion that the mind of a first-century Palestinian Jew would be a more adequate medium for these purposes than, say, the mind of a twentieth-century English physicist, chastening as it may be for us to accept this; the concept of the Servant of Jahweh may be more fruitful religiously than that of the neutrino. Père Bouyer has posited the question 'How can the fact that the Son of God has become man . . . *in an individual* of our history, Jesus of Nazareth, concern us *all*, to the point that the salvation of us all depends on it and has been made possible by that alone that Jesus has done among us?' and has commented: 'That is, down to the present day, *the* Christological question; it is inevitable and yet unsolved.'[2] With all respect to one of the profoundest of living theologians, I would suggest that perhaps the fact that the coeternal and consubstantial Son of God should become a first-century Jew is not primarily a *problem* for *Christology*; it is rather its *presupposition*. So far from needing to be explained, it is the explanation of everything else. Profoundly mysterious as the union of manhood with God in the Incarnate Son must inevitably be to our finite and clouded minds, it is in itself the most luminous and illuminating of realities. I would repeat that it is the literal assumption of a complete human nature by the unchanged Son of God that makes Christology genuinely intelligible, while the various deviant attempts, from Apollinarius onwards, to produce a more easily acceptable figure by minimizing one or other of the terms inevitably end up in increased obscurity and reduced efficacy. In contrast, Chalcedonian orthodoxy holds together in unstrained unity and coherence both the particularity of Jesus the Jew of Nazareth and the universality of the incarnate Word, the creator and redeemer of mankind. The precise and detailed conditions under which the Eternal Word will be manifested in human nature are hardly open to purely theoretical speculation, or perhaps it would be more accurate to say that, while they are open to, and are a legitimate field for, theoretical speculation, theoretical speculation is unlikely to give us very reliable conclusions. These are rather a matter to be known, in so far as they *are* known, by divine revelation, as embodied in Scripture and interpreted in the tradition and experience of the Church. I sympathize with Fr Rahner's complaint, in one of his pre-conciliar writings, against the Christology of the scholastic manuals, that 'the only texts from Scripture, whether they are sayings of Christ himself or appear in the teaching of the Apostles in which it is interested are those which can be translated as directly as possible in the terms of classical metaphysical Christology.' 'The method is a legitimate one;' he continued, 'but it cannot cover the whole ground. A whole body of Christological statements remains unused in this way, statements which describe Jesus' relationship to the Father (God) in the categories proper to conscious experience (existentially): Jesus as the only one to know the Father, Jesus who brings tidings of him, does his will at all times, is always heard by him and so on.'[3] On the other hand, as Dr Flesseman-van Leer pointed out to her former teacher Professor C. F. Evans,[4] it is no less easy for the modern New-Testament critic to get so carried away by the application of more and more sophisticated types of scriptural analysis (the latest, coming after a century of source-, form- and redaction-criticism appears to be known as 'structural exegesis') that the serious study of the sacred text becomes the monopoly of a specially trained élite, and the warm human realism of the Gospels and Epistles, which has endeared them to Christian readers down the centuries, is virtually lost from view. It must be stressed that those very characteristics of human thinking and knowing on the part of Jesus which the 'liberal' Christologist can only categorize in terms of ignorance and error are, from the standpoint of authentic Chalcedonianism, the conditions of God's own presence and self-revelation in a human life. Furthermore—and this is a point where Chalcedon points us beyond, though certainly not against, its own explicit teaching—since human nature, in any individual, is not given from its beginning in a fully developed state but develops from the unrealized potentialities of the original fertilized ovum through birth, infancy, childhood, and adolescence to its climax in adult manhood, we must surely hold that the mentality of Jesus, like that of any other human being, developed *pari passu* with the development of his bodily organism. To say this is not to imply that it was in any way defective in the early stages; on the contrary, at each stage it was precisely what at that stage it is proper for human nature to be. It is surely a valid insight that asserts that you must not try to put an old head on young shoulders. It is not simply a discovery of modern anthropology that mental and physical (especially cerebral) functioning are intimately and intricately allied; it is inherent in the traditional Christian belief that a human being is not a pure spirit temporarily incapsulated in a body but is a bipartite psychophysical unity. It is therefore astonishing that many theologians have taken it for granted that if Jesus was both God and man his human mind must have contained, from the first moment of his existence, a replica of the divine omniscience, so that, even in the womb of Mary, he was solving differential equations and designing nuclear reactors. Nothing as crude as this is, of course, to be found in a great thinker like St Thomas Aquinas, and his most recent editor has remarked that, paradoxical as it will appear to contemporary theologians and exegetes, the elaborate structure which he ascribes to Christ's knowledge was worked out precisely in order to safeguard the reality of the Saviour's humanity.[5] Nevertheless, both the psychological and the physiological information that were available to the Angelic Doctor in the thirteenth century are now seen to be grossly inadequate. A modern discussion of Jesus' human knowledge will need to take account of all that is now known about the psychophysical structure of the cognitive process and about the development of human mentality from its beginning in the fertilized ovum to its culmination in adulthood. That this must be done on the *theological* basis of orthodox Chalcedonian Christology will in fact be not a restriction but a liberation. Two warnings need, however, to be kept in mind. The first is the general reminder that even the twentieth-century scientific beliefs are subject to revision and will almost certainly receive it. The second is the theological point that, while Jesus' human nature is more and not less genuinely human for its assumption by the person of the eternal Son of God, it may for that very reason be expected to manifest powers and capacities which outstrip those of human nature as we normally experience it both in ourselves and in others. Some of these powers and capacities may pertain to Jesus simply because his human nature is unfallen and perfect, whereas ours is fallen and maimed and, though redeemed, is still in process of recreation and restoration. Others may pertain to it because its person is the divine Word, because 'in him the whole fullness of deity dwells bodily'.[6] It may be difficult to discriminate in any given case between these alternatives; nor, I think, will it greatly matter, provided we keep a firm grasp upon the principle that, even in the supreme example of the incarnation, grace does not suppress nature but perfects it. As instances of the kind of discussion that I have in mind I will just mention two which can be found in my recent book *Theology and the Gospel of Christ*. The first is concerned with the relation between modern genetic theory and the virginal conception of Jesus, the second with the moment at which a rational human soul appeared in his embryonic body.[7] A further and, as far as I know, an unexplored field for investigation, in which the supernatural and natural orders are mutually involved in a supremely intimate and delicate way, is that of the transformation undergone by the human nature of Jesus, and particularly by his body, at his resurrection. In this connection it is interesting to observe that, throughout the mass of theological controversy and scientific investigation that has grown up during the present century around the Holy Shroud of Turin, it has never been suggested, even by the most conservative ecclesiastics, that there was anything either inherently irreverent or futile in the use of all available and relevant methods of physical, chemical, and biological science in studying the impression of a human figure which is visible on the fabric of the relic. Even if the ultimate explanation of the phenomenon is supernatural and there is a point beyond which the techniques and insights of natural science cannot take us, nevertheless—the assumption is plain—it is both legitimate and useful for us to follow those techniques and insights up to the point beyond which they cannot go.[8] For—once again the principle is valid—grace perfects nature and does not destroy it, and grace and nature are alike under the creative providence of the same God.

CHALCEDON IN A WIDER CONTEXT

A very different direction in which the Chalcedonian Christology calls for amplification and development is that of the relation of the incarnation to the human race as a whole and, beyond that, to the rest of the material universe. It has been generally recognized by Christian thinkers that the history of the human race in general and that of the Jewish people in particular has been, under divine providence, a gradually converging process whose culmination was the overshadowing by the Holy Spirit of a particular young woman so that she might be the human mother of the divine and pre-existent Son of God. It is this that provides the justification for the use of the Jewish scriptures in Christian liturgy and devotion and that gives the ground for a Mariology which is soundly theological, free from sentimentality, and organically integrated into the whole body of Christian truth. It is as basic to the Protestant Max Thurian's book *Marie, Mère du Seigneur, Figure de l'Eglise*[1] as to the Marian chapter of the Decree of Vatican II on the Church[2] and its sequel in the Apostolic Exhortation *Marialis Cultus* of Pope Paul VI. It is this renewed emphasis on the fact, made plain by both Ephesus and Chalcedon, that the supreme theological truth about Mary is that she is *Theotokos*, the Mother of God, whose son is of the very same substance as us in his manhood, that has rescued Mariology from the apparently uncontrollable hypertrophy of the preconciliar years. The notion that the redemptive activity of God (*Heilsgeschichte*) was, with many divagations and setbacks, gradually focused down through the history of the Jewish people to its climactic convergence and concentration in the twofold figure of Mary and her Son, and then spread out from that focal point into the whole world under the form of Christ's Spirit-endowed body the Catholic Church—this noble and inspiring notion has been part of the equipment of Christian tradition from the beginning. It is implicit in the Pauline epistles and was splendidly developed by St Irenaeus, though it has sometimes fallen into the background, especially in the West.[3] It has maintained itself far more strongly in the Christian East, where it has been set in an even larger context and given even wider implications. Very prominent in the Orthodox liturgy is the sense that the assumption of human nature by the person of the divine Word has had repercussions throughout the human race and indeed, beyond the human race, throughout the material universe. The whole of the material order is seen as in principle transfigured and transformed by the taking of a material body by the Son of God, and the Feast of the Transfiguration of Christ is seen as the feast of the transfiguration of the whole of the physical world. Thus the Russian theologian Paul Evdokimov has written:

The formation of Christ in man, his Christification, is neither an impossible imitation nor the application to man of the merits of the Incarnation, but is *the injection into man of the*

Incarnation itself, and it is brought about and perpetuated by the Eucharistic Mystery.[4]

I have discussed this theme in some detail in my Boyle Lectures *The Christian Universe*,[5] especially in the form which it took with Père Pierre Teilhard de Chardin. It clearly presupposes the strictest Chalcedonian orthodoxy. I would comment—and I do not think Evdokimov would have disagreed—that if, in the Eucharistic Mystery, the incarnation itself is injected into man, this is possible only because, in the incarnation, God has injected himself into the human race, an act which, in the words of that very Western document *Quicunque vult*, took place, not by the conversion of Godhead into flesh, but by the assumption of manhood into God. In Teilhard's magnificent words, 'Christ invests himself organically with the very majesty of his creation.'[6] And I wish to suggest, without in the least subtracting from the unique and supreme status and function of Jesus and Mary in the economy of man's redemption, but rather as a consequence of them, that the eternal Word's investiture of himself with manhood in the womb of Mary produced not just a transitory repercussion throughout the human race but a real and permanent change in humanity itself. Human nature has never been the same since God became man, for, in the words of one of the recent editors of St Thomas Aquinas, 'the central point of Christian belief is that the maker of the universe is *now* a man.'[7] What this should imply for the interpretation of human history outside the *praeparatio evangelica* of Judaism, for the evaluation of the non-Christian religions, and for the understanding of human behaviour in general are matters needing careful and co-operative discussion in which others as well as theologians should be involved. All that I wish to do here is to draw attention to an important factor which in the vast mass of material that has been produced on these topics has been almost invariably ignored. Sometimes careful comparisons are made between the doctrines of the various world-religions, their cultural outlooks and their ethical principles. Sometimes the question is asked about the way in which the immanent Logos, 'the light that lightens every man coming into the world', may be supposed to have illuminated the minds of sincere followers of this or that non-Christian faith, a question which need not presuppose more than the vaguest type of theism or quasi-theism. It is by no means to be despised as futile or excluded as illegitimate. But I wish to suggest that for Christians there is a more important question which is much less frequently raised, namely this: What, in view of the fact that he has been a man for almost the last two thousand years, can we judge that the Incarnate Son of God has been doing all that time, and is doing today, in this or that non-Christian religion? For one great living religious culture, this question has been broached by Fr Raymond Panikkar in his book *The Unknown Christ of Hinduism*,[8] but much more work is needed on these lines. It demands as its presupposition the full Chalcedonian doctrine of the incarnation, with its closely integrated union of Godhead and manhood, of universality and particularity, in Jesus the Saviour of Mankind. It demands more than Mr Don Cupitt's vision of Christianity as 'a family of monotheistic faiths which in various ways find in Jesus a key to the relation of man with God',[9] more than Dr John Hick's picture of the future as 'one in which what we now call different religions will constitute the past history of different emphases and variations within something that it need not be too misleading to call a single world religion'[10] and more than Dr D. E. Nineham's even more radical questioning whether it is 'any longer worthwhile to attempt to trace the Christian's ever-changing understanding of his relationship with God directly back to some identifiable element in the life, character and activity of Jesus of Nazareth.'[11] On the other hand, it also implies a much more realistic view of the unity of the human species on the theological level than human nature would enjoy simply as an Aristotelian universal. Indeed, I doubt whether this unity can be fully and adequately expressed in the concepts of any philosophical system whatever, useful as some of them may be within their limits and in their special ways; this is why, in the last sentence, I inserted the word 'theological'. Certainly it will not do simply to substitute a Platonic for an Aristotelian view of universals; for the Platonic universals were alleged to exist in an ideal realm of forms, uncontaminated by our earthly in-involvement in time and matter, whereas the manhood which the Eternal assumed and redeemed is that of the Toms, Dicks, and Harrys, the Aurungszebes, Heliogabaluses, Valentinos, Nefertitis, Adelaides, and Marlenes, and other less colourful figures, who make up the actual human race. It may well be the case that the redemption of mankind by and in Christ has revealed that mankind possesses a unity which cannot be adequately systematized in the terms of any secular thought-system, philosophical, psychological, biological, or any other, but only in strictly theological terms, though it will have its repercussions in all those other fields. (This kind of situation has occurred before in the history of Christendom, and not least in the work of St Thomas Aquinas. Aristotelian though he was, he refused to admit that the Supreme Being was an altogether remote unmoved mover, concerned only with his own perfection and exercising no genuine efficient causality upon the world; while accepting Aristotle's arguments for what they were worth, he insisted that they led to a Judaeo-Christian and not an Aristotelian God. And he did nothing less than violence to the doctrine of the individuation of forms by matter in order to maintain our personal survival of bodily death.) Here, then, is a field—that of missiology and of the study of the non-Christian religions—to which Chalcedonian Christology, if taken seriously, will have a vast contribution to make. And there are other human disciplines in which intelligent Christian judgement (which is something different from benevolent Christian moralizing) will have a distinctive insight to offer, in the light of the truth that the Creator of the universe is now a member of the human race. Sociology and politics are obvious examples.

I should here interject, to remove possible fears and misunderstandings, that, if we hold that a real and radical change has been brought about in the human race by the simple fact that God has become man, we do not imply that the Church has been mistaken in its insistence upon the real and radical change that it has alleged takes place in the sacrament of Christian initiation and in the whole fabric of sacramental life in the Body of Christ that follows upon it. For, to do no more that touch upon a theme whose detailed elaboration would need very careful and extensive theological consideration, there is surely nothing repugnant in holding that the grace which the Son of God communicated to the human race by becoming himself a member of it is not totally withheld from each of its members until he is sacramentally incorporated into the visible Church. May we not rather see Christian initiation as the crowning with fresh grace of the grace already given to us in the incarnation itself? We are, I suggest, the victims of needless timidity if we write off as merely imaginative or rhetorical the language in which many of the Eastern fathers have seen the human race redeemed and transformed from the moment when the eternal Word was enfleshed within it. I should, in fact, expect the line of thought which I have been commending, and which is in its inspiration uncompromisingly Chalcedonian, to have very significant consequences for ecclesiology and sacramental theology and to reinforce rather than to undermine their own importance.

But what, it may now be objected, if man is not the only rational species in the material universe? If, as has been estimated, the number of extra-galactic nebulae runs into hundreds of millions and if any one of these may contain a hundred thousand million stars and if many of these stars may have planets comparable with our own earth, need we dogmatically deny the possibility that there may be other rational species than ours? Is such a possibility difficult to reconcile with Christian orthodoxy? I discussed this question more than twenty years ago in my book *Christian Theology and Natural Science*[12] at considerable length. For the details of my argument I must refer the reader to that work. Here I will merely reiterate the conclusion to which I came and which still seems to me to be sound:

> There may or may not be somewhere in the universe rational beings other than man. If there are, they may or may not have fallen. If they have fallen, their redemption may or may not require that the Son of God should become incarnate in their nature. God may or may not have some other way of restoring them to fellowship with himself; he may perhaps have an even more wonderful way, of which we cannot form the remotest conception. Whatever may be the truth about this, . . . I cannot see any conclusive theological objection to the view that the divine Word may have become incarnate in other rational species than our own.[13]

I must, however, stress that this possibility of an incarnation of the divine Word in more than one rational species depends very much upon incarnation being conceived on the Chalcedonian pattern, as the assumption of a created rational nature by the

51

immutable uncreated person of the Word. It is altogether unthinkable in a Christology of the kenotic type, according to which each incarnation would involve a scaling down or amputation of the divine nature for a temporary period in a different way. Such speculation as this is bound to be inconclusive, if only because of the hypothetical character of the circumstances in which it is operating. It may nevertheless not be altogether useless. For, if I may quote myself again:

> It has perhaps shown how wide is the liberty that Christian orthodoxy leaves to intellectual speculation, and how many are the avenues that it opens up. Theological principles tend to become torpid for lack of exercise, and there is much to be said for giving them now and then a scamper in a field where the paths are few and the boundaries undefined; they do their day-by-day work all the better for an occasional outing in the country. Outings, however, are outings and work is work, and it is very important not to confuse them with each other.[14]

CHALCEDON AND THE FUTURE

There are other areas of theology, and other problems within them, than those upon which I have touched, and of the latter some might usefully have received much fuller discussion than I have given them. I have, however, tried to show, by taking some specific topics, that, in addition to the supremely important characteristics of intelligibility and truth, the Chalcedonian Christology has the further characteristics needed by any theological doctrine which can hope to survive, namely fertility and flexibility. By fertility, I mean that it must be able to contribute constructively and creatively to the solution of problems that did not exist, or were not consciously recognized, when it was first formulated; by flexibility I mean that, while it must not hastily and timidly capitulate to every fashion and pressure of the circumambient culture, it must be sensitive to unfamiliar needs and attitudes and responsive to new discoveries and insights. In both these respects, and in the all-important task of preserving the balance between them, the Christology of Chalcedon is far more successful than those of the various 'New Theologies' that have successively clamoured for acceptance. So far from Chalcedon having run into a dead-end or outlasted its usefulness, I believe it may have greater possibilities of achievement awaiting it in our modern age.

Additional Note A:
Incarnation and Sonship

In the chapter on Christology in my recent book *Theology and the Gospel of Christ*[1] I have stressed the importance of the fact that in Jesus it is not just *God*, but *God the Son*, who has become man and have shown, with special reference to Père Louis Bouyer and Père Jean Galot, the implications of this for the much discussed question of the self-consciousness of Jesus. The relevant passages are the following. From Bouyer:

> We must not try to represent to ourselves this consciousness of Jesus, whether messianic or filial, as being essentially, and still less as being primarily, a reflex consciousness of its own identity. . . . All the difficulties which that starting-point cannot avoid accumulating vanish as soon as we recognize that this consciousness of Jesus, like every normal consciousness, was the consciousness of an object before becoming a consciousness of its own subject. The consciousness of Jesus, as the human consciousness of the Son of God, was before all else consciousness *of God*. Jesus was 'the Christ, the Son of the living God', not directly by knowing that he was, but because he knew God *as the Father*, with everything of the unique and the ineffable that that means for him according to the Gospel.[2]

And from Galot:

> It is this [sc. *Abba*] that is the most apt term to indicate to us how the consciousness of divine sonship was formed in Jesus. We have seen that the *Ego eimi* is used by Jesus only in the perspective of a fundamental relation to the Father; and the key to the significance of this *Ego eimi* is found in the word *Abba*. Similarly, the declarations about the Son of Man imply a mysterious sonship in Jesus of divine origin; the force of this title can be further unveiled only by reference to the term *Abba*. The name *Abba* thus has a primordial force which illuminates all the expressions of the consciousness of Jesus.

No other term could have been as meaningful to witness to the point at which the consciousness of divine sonship is, in Jesus, a consciousness that is perfectly human. *Abba* is the term used by someone who has a consciousness like that of other children, but with this difference, that in this case the father is not a human father, but is God.[3]

Mr Brian Hebblethwaite has drawn attention, in a recent article,[4] to a striking passage in which, with his characteristic evocative power, the late Austin Farrer made the same point in a sermon:

We cannot understand Jesus as simply the God-who-was-man. We have left out an essential factor, the sonship. Jesus is not simply God manifest as man; he is the divine Son coming in manhood. What was expressed in human terms here below was not bare deity; it was divine sonship. God cannot live an identically godlike life in eternity and in a human story. But the divine Son can make an identical response to his Father, whether in the love of the blessed Trinity or in the fulfilment of an earthly ministry. All the conditions of action are different on the two levels; the filial response is one. Above, the appropriate response is a co-operation in sovereignty and an interchange of eternal joys. Then the Son gives back to the Father all that the Father is. Below, in the incarnate life, the appropriate response is an obedience to inspiration, a waiting for direction, an acceptance of suffering, a rectitude of choice, a resistance to temptation, a willingness to die. For such things are the stuff of our existence; and it was in this very stuff that Christ worked out the theme of heavenly sonship, proving himself on earth the very thing he was in heaven; that is, a continual perfect act of filial love.[5]

Mr Hebblethwaite comments that Farrer was quite right to see the relation of Jesus to the Father as reflecting an inner-trinitarian relation and that, as far as Jesus was concerned, that relation was bound to express itself in terms of mission and dependence. But, he adds, 'to see this as reflecting eternal derivedness or filiation in the Trinity is perhaps to go too far'; it reminds him of the 'residual subordinationism' which Leonard Hodgson firmly rejected in his book *The Doctrine of the*

Trinity. I should want to reply that derivedness does not necessarily imply subordination and that, as I argued in my small book *Via Media*,[6] it was the great contribution of the Council of Nicaea to make it plain that there could be a coherent concept of *derived equality*. However, I agree that, when the relation of filiality is reflected on to the created level in the incarnation it appears there in a subordinate mode; in the words of *Quicunque vult*, 'Our Lord Jesus Christ, the Son of God, . . . is equal to the Father in respect of his divinity and less than the Father in respect of his humanity'. On this particular point, then, I think Farrer was right and Hebblethwaite was mistaken; on all other aspects of the incarnation they appear to be in complete accord. Mr Hebblethwaite deserves our gratitude for the assiduity with which he has combed Farrer's voluminous works and the penetration with which he has assessed the results of his combing. 'There can be little doubt', he concludes, 'that what Farrer is expounding here is the central tenet of historic Christianity, nor that Farrer's lucid and profound exposition helps us to see the religious significance and force of incarnational belief.'[7] And I would echo his hope that '[Farrer's] words will also help us to see that the doctrine of the Incarnation really is a matter of insight rather than illusion.'[8]

Additional Note B:
Dr Moule on the Origin of Christology

Dr C. F. D. Moule, who recently retired from the Lady Margaret Chair of Divinity at Cambridge, is one of the most learned and judicious of contemporary New-Testament scholars—and also one of the most readable. In 1967 he published a short work entitled *The Phenomenon of the New Testament*,[1] which he described as 'An enquiry into the implications of certain features of the New Testament'. In spite of its brevity, which caused it to make perhaps less impact in scholarly circles than it deserved, it was both original and impressive. It was the product of a conviction that the existence of the New Testament, and still more the existence of the society in which it was born, posed certain questions which demanded to be answered but which were very commonly ignored or evaded.

All I am trying to do [Dr Moule wrote] is to present certain undoubted phenomena of the New Testament writings and to ask how the reader proposes to account for them. If the coming into existence of the Nazarenes, a phenomenon undeniably attested by the New Testament, rips a great hole in history, a hole of the size and shape of Resurrection, what does the secular historian propose to stop it up with? If a Jewish writer like Paul speaks of a contemporary, Jesus of Nazareth, in language up to that time used only in reference to great symbolic figures of the remote past, what account are we to give of the process leading to this? And so forth. It seems to me that opponents of Christianity are allowed too easily either to avoid such questions altogether or to get round them with shallow speculations which do not really survive scrutiny. It is phenomena of this sort that I propose to examine, inviting interested students to join in the examination and then to talk about it with others.[2]

Against the view that what differentiated Christianity from other religious movements was its special ethical teaching, Moule replied that

the one really distinctive thing for which the Christians stood was their declaration that Jesus had been raised from the dead according to God's design, and the consequent estimate of him as in a unique sense Son of God and representative man, and the resulting conception of the way to reconciliation.[3]

'Thus,' he asserted,

all the evidence converges on the conclusion—so far as I can see—that there was nothing to discriminate Christians initially from any other Jews of their day except their convictions about Jesus; and that it was these which kept them from lapsing back into Judaism, or, rather, which ultimately forced them out of Judaism; which means either that these convictions were justified or else, if they were not, that the rise and continuance of the Christian Church still await explanation.[4]

And the final result to which he came, after a detailed examination of those aspects of the New-Testament phenomenon which seemed to him to call most inescapably for explanation, was summed up in these three propositions:

First, whoever tries to account for the beginnings of Christianity by some purely historical, non-transcendental event, runs up against the difficulty that there seems to be no such event of sufficient magnitude or of a kind such as to fulfil the need. . . .

Secondly, whoever tries to interpret Jesus as only an individual of past history, instead of as a somehow inclusive being, is confronted by phenomena of language and experience whose origin then defies explanation.

Thirdly . . ., whoever deems that the conception of Jesus as standing in a unique relation to God is a figment of pious imagination, must explain how it came to be constructed, with almost inconceivable and apparently unpremeditated ingenuity, so as to be to such a degree coherent and subtly consistent with itself.[5]

Taking up the substantial position, though not accepting all the details, of the celebrated work *The Riddle of the New Testament*,[6] which appeared from E. C. Hoskyns and F. N. Davey in 1931, Moule maintained that 'the nearer you push the inquiry back to the original Jesus, the more you find that you cannot have him without a transcendental element.'[7] Writing as he was in 1967, he diagnosed the apologetic situation as follows:

It seems to me that we stand today once more at the parting of the ways. Recent theological writing has tended to dismiss the importance of history in favour of the transcendental call to decision; or, alternatively, to dismiss the transcendent in favour of such history as can be confined within the categories of purely human comprehension. But I cannot see how a serious student of Christian origins can concur with either.[8]

Ten years later, in 1977, there was published Dr Moule's book *The Origin of Christology*.[9] While modestly limiting his scope to his special expertise as a New-Testament scholar, he stressed its concern with 'matters of contemporary urgency'. 'Indeed,' he wrote,

it is, in a sense, a reply to a contemporary challenge. . . . The main impetus behind these studies is the
conviction, slowly generated over the years, that there are
unexamined false assumptions behind a good deal of contemporary New Testament scholarship. Of these the one I
have particularly in mind is the assumption that the genesis
of Christology . . . can be explained as a sort of evolutionary
process, in the manner of the so-called 'history of religions
school' of thought.[10]

Nothing is now said, we may notice, about any 'parting of the
ways' or about transcendental decisions; these are indeed in
evidence on the level of church life, and especially in conservative evangelical circles, but academic theology, at least in
the English-speaking world, has moved steadily since 1967
towards 'the categories of purely human comprehension'. We
are now in the year of *The Myth of God Incarnate*,[11] and indeed
Dr Moule's book is to be considered, if not as a specific reply to
that book, at least as a reply to the attitude that gave it birth.
For, chief among the false assumptions which Dr Moule attacks
is the assumption that, under the influence of non-Semitic
saviour-cults, the Church came to substitute the acclamation of
Jesus as a divine Lord for its original invocation of him as a
revered Master. On the contrary, argues Dr Moule,

the various estimates of Jesus reflected in the New Testament
[are], in essence, only attempts to describe what was already
there from the beginning. They are not successive additions
of something new, but only the drawing out and articulating
of what is there. They represent various stages in the
development of perception, but they do not represent the
accretion of any alien factors that were not inherent from the
beginning.[12]

In building up his case, Dr Moule successively examines in
detail (1) four 'titles' of Jesus (the Son of Man, the Son of God,
Christ, and *Kurios*), (2) the notion of Christ as 'corporate',
(3) non-Pauline conceptions, (4) the scope of Christ's death,
and (5) the theme of 'fulfilment', all in their New-Testament
understanding and development. He reprints from the journal
Theology[13] a controversy which he had with Dr Haddon
Willmer about the 'ultimacy' and 'distinctiveness' of Christ.

On the much discussed theme of the personal pre-existence of Jesus he sees the resurrection as determinative:

> I want to say not only that, 'as a result of him', they experienced a new world; but that they experienced Jesus himself as in a dimension transcending the human and the temporal. It is not just that owing (somehow) to Jesus, they found new life; it is that they discovered in Jesus himself, alive and present, a divine dimension such that he must always and eternally have existed in it. [14]

And again:

> A person who had recently been crucified, but is found to be alive, with 'absolute' life, the life of the age to come, and is found, moreover, to be an inclusive, all-embracing presence—such a person is beginning to be described in terms appropriate to nothing less than God himself. [15]

In the concluding 'Prospect', in which the issue of 'ultimacy' is raised, Dr Moule realistically and refreshingly observes that 'the New Testament specialist cannot be content to stay within his own field for ever', [16] while he modestly affirms that he asks certain questions unashamedly only because every Christian has to ask them and that he includes them only as a bridge to what lies beyond his own expert study. Among these he inquires whether and, if so, in what way our increasing knowledge about man, psychologically and sociologically, manifests only a developing insight into what has, all along, been given 'in Christ', and what are the Christological implications of the possibility that man is not the only rational being in the material universe and of the possibility that, on this earth, man may evolve into a new species. [17] And, reluctant as he is to overstep the boundaries of his own territory, I think the plain implication of his study is this, that it is a Christology of the assumption of human nature by the pre-existent Son of God, and not a Christology of the gradual apotheosis of a revered teacher by his followers, that not only is true to the New-Testament evidence itself, but also makes Christianity relevant to human life and culture in general and to the insights and problems of our own time in particular.

The Origin of Christology is an extremely important book—and a timely one.

Additional Note C:
The Shroud of Turin

It is difficult to trace the history of this remarkable relic farther
back than the later part of the fourteenth century, though an
impressive case has been made out by Mr Ian Wilson for its
identification with the object known as the Mandylion, which
was transferred from Edessa to Constantinople in A.D. 944,
whence it disappeared during the sack of the city by the Cru-
saders in 1204. In 1353 a church was founded for the veneration
of the Shroud at Lirey in France and it was at one time the
subject of a dispute between the Canons of Lirey and the Bishop
of Troyes, who denounced it as a forgery. It passed from the
local de Charney family into the possession of the Dukes of
Savoy, and now, as the property of King Umberto, it is housed
in a very beautiful seventeenth-century chapel, completed by
Guarino Guarini, adjacent to the cathedral in Turin. Astonishing as this may seem, it bears every sign of being the actual
cloth in which the body of Jesus of Nazareth was placed at his
burial.

The widespread modern interest in it began with the discovery, when it was first photographed in 1898, that the impression of the body which was faintly visible on the fabric had the
form of a photographic negative, a feature which no medieval
forger could conceivably have tried to produce or have suc-
ceeded in producing if he had tried. Later study of the image
and the cloth, based on further examination in 1931 and 1933,
revealed a number of other features which agree with modern
historical and scientific knowledge but would have been totally
outside the concepts and the capacities of any supposed
counterfeiter. Still further scientific examination was allowed in
1969 and 1973 and the results have been published. At the
time of writing (January 1979) the most comprehensive and
detailed account of the *status quaestionis* is provided by the
published *Proceedings of the 1977 United States Conference of
Research on the Shroud of Turin*,[1] but a very readable and in-
formative short article by Dr J. A. T. Robinson appeared in
Theology in May 1977.[2] The total amount of literature, of very
varied quality, on the Shroud is very large indeed.

The upshot of this whole movement of research, made with
more and more refined and sophisticated methods, can be

stated quite simply. It is this, that all the evidence is consistent with the Shroud having contained the body of Jesus, scourged and crucified in the manner described in the Gospels and removed, whether by natural or supernatural means, a short while after death. Every fresh refinement of research has simply brought to light fresh details consistent both with the Gospel account and with modern historical and scientific method, and none of the new discoveries has in any way contradicted the traditional views. As a speaker said at a recent conference in London, if the Shroud did not contain the body of Jesus, it must have contained the body of someone who had been first scourged and then crucified in a way that was a detailed and deliberate imitation of his passion, and who was then buried in the precise way in which he himself had been buried. And this seems frankly incredible. In the epigrammatic words of a scholar whose attitude to early relics is in general sceptical, everything would seem to be against the authenticity of the Shroud—except the evidence. This is definitely not one of those dubious relics of which Bishop García Martínez declared at Vatican II, *Reverenter sepeliantur et deinceps nulla mentio fiat.*[3]

One of the most fascinating aspects of this whole affair is the vast number and the variety of the·fields of research that have been involved; more, one may well imagine, than in any other research project. Biblical scholars, Roman and medieval historians, physiologists, physicists, chemists, computer mathematicians, and even pollen experts have collaborated. Such highly sophisticated methods as X-ray fluorescence analysis, infra-red thermography, diffusion analysis, colour analysis, computer-aided image-enhancement, and the reconstruction of three-dimensional objects from their two-dimensional projections have all been brought together in a co-operative interdisciplinary endeavour ultimately activated by Christian belief. Some of the most interesting work has been done in their spare time by members of the United States Air Force Academy, applying to Shroud-study the space-programme technology associated with such projects as the photography of the planet Mars. A very readable account is given by the Revd H. David Sox in his book *File on the Shroud*,[4] and the latest tests, made at the time of the exposition in October 1978, are described by the same author in an article in *The Tablet.*[5] One unexpected development is the interest now being shown in sindonology by Jews, Mohammedans, and, indeed, atheists, including members of the Ahmadiyya Movement in Islam, who hold that Jesus survived his crucifixion and that his true sepulchre is in Srinagar, Kashmir.

There seems in fact to be no reasonable doubt that the serene and awe-inspiring countenance which the experts have discerned in the figure on the Shroud is in fact Jesus of Nazareth. The Shroud has already brought about much genuine deepening and intensification of devotion among those to whom knowledge of it has come, and those may be right who believe the Shroud to be one of God's great gifts to the Church, to restore and increase faith at a time when life and thought have become progressively secularized. But some cautions need to be borne in mind.

The truth of the Christian religion does not in any way depend on the authenticity of the Shroud. Christian belief was intelligently held and devoutly practised before the Shroud was recognized, and if the Shroud should, in spite of all appearances, turn out to be a forgery, our faith would be unaffected. No Christian creed contains the clause 'I believe in the Shroud of Turin'. Secondly, however moving it may be to have before us the true and genuine representation of the Lord, imprinted by no human or even angelic hand but by his own very body, it must not be forgotten that what is depicted there is the dead Christ, though indeed on the verge of his resurrection. And in the Church, which too is his body, and supremely in the Sacrament of the Eucharist, we meet not with an image of the dead Christ but with the actual presence of the living and risen Christ, not merely to be gazed on but to be our food and our life. What the Shroud can do is to remind us of the literal reality of the incarnation, of the fact that, in Jesus, God the Son has taken human nature in its concrete totality, body no less than soul, and that in that body he has literally undergone a human death: *crucifixus, mortuus et sepultus*, says the Creed. The Shroud leaves us with many questions to which we do not know, and perhaps will never fully know, the answers. What is the process, chemical, radiative, or whatever, by which the image was imprinted on the fabric? What is the actual chemical constitution of the image? Is it a deposit on the fabric or a chemical modification of it? What was, in terms of physics and biology, the nature of the change that Christ's body underwent at the resurrection? Did he pass through the fabric of the Shroud or step out from it? And, enveloping all such questions, is the omnibus question: just in what way are the natural and supernatural factors related in the great act of the Lord's resurrection? Here there is much room for speculation, and in our speculation, while holding firmly to the truth that the resurrection is a supernatural act whose agent is the living God, we must hold equally firmly to the basic Catholic principle that grace neither destroys nor rejects nor ignores nature, but fulfils and perfects and transforms it. And, as I pointed out in the text, it is very significant that, in all the discussions that the Shroud has provoked, it has never been suggested, even by the most strictly traditional scholars, that the laws which normally apply to human bodies were irrelevant to the body of Jesus, inadequate as they are to describe his full reality. For— though this often appears to be forgotten—it is just as much a truth of the Catholic faith that Jesus is fully and completely man as that he is fully and completely God: *Theon alēthōs kai anthrōpon alēthōs*, insists Chalcedon. This cannot be too strongly emphasized at a time when we have so often to affirm the deity of Jesus against those who deny it. The truth of God incarnate implies indeed that he is God; it implies no less than he is man, for that is what 'incarnate' means. We must not allow the manhood of Jesus to become the monopoly of those who deny that he is God. This is perhaps the chief lesson that the Shroud has to teach us.

3 *Suffering and God:*
Passion, Compassion, and Impassibility

Popule meus, quid feci tibi? aut in quo contristavi te?
Responde mihi
Liturgy of Good Friday

CHANGE AND BECOMING:
FR WEINANDY'S ANALYSIS

It was the great achievement of the Council of Chalcedon that, in making it plain that the person of Jesus of Nazareth is none other than the eternal Son and Word of God, the Second Person of the Holy Trinity, and that he is the subject of two complete, distinct, and unconfused yet inseparable natures, the one divine and the other human, it satisfied, without embarrassment or evasiveness, the two essential requirements for any satisfactory Christology. The first of these is the recognition, in Jesus, of a fully concrete human organism, lacking nothing in either its bodily or its mental aspect, in which he has lived an authentically human life and has undergone, literally and not just metaphorically or in appearance, the sufferings of crucifixion and death; the second is that God himself is involved, personally and not merely by sympathy or complacency, as the subject of these human experiences. Thus, by providing the eternal Word with a human nature that can undergo suffering, Chalcedonian orthodoxy makes it possible for the eternal Word, who is absolutely impassible and immutable in his Godhead, to be really and literally passible and mutable in his manhood. It is in his manhood that he suffers, but he who suffers in it is God.

I have already stressed the importance of maintaining that person, *hypostasis*, is not a *part* of nature, not even a tiny and indetectible part, but is its *subject*; and I have remarked that, although at first sight this may seem to be a technical subtlety, it is no more than is implied by the plain language of the Creeds.[1] Without it we shall either attribute to Jesus something less than a genuine and integral human life or we shall see his human life as lived by someone who is other than, and less

64

than, God. It will be helpful to illustrate this from a brilliant, but as yet unpublished, thesis, to which I have briefly referred elsewhere,[2] by Dr Thomas G. Weinandy, OFMCap, on 'The Immutability and Impassibility of God with reference to the Doctrine of the Incarnation'.[3]

Weinandy's guiding principle throughout his investigation—and a very fruitful and illuminating principle it proved to be—is that the key to any Christology lies in the understanding which its proponents have of the notion of *becoming* in the basic Christological formula 'The Word became flesh' or, from Nicaea onwards, 'God became man'. He begins by making a survey of the development of Christology from the New Testament to Chalcedon. This has, of course, been done many times before, but his purpose is to show that this development culminates in the view of becoming which he denotes as 'Personal/Existential' and describes in these words:

> Because the Council Fathers [of Chalcedon] understand Christ to be the one person of the Logos existing in two ways, as God and as man, one can see that, like Cyril, they do not understand 'become' in a way that implies a change of natures. The Logos does not change his nature, what he is, from God to man. Nor does what he becomes, man, change in some way into the nature of God. Rather Chalcedon understands 'become' as an existential/personal concept denoting that the Logos *has come to be man.* Chalcedon even rids this understanding of Cyril's ambiguity. The Council in opting for 'in two natures' rather than 'out of two natures' clarifies the fact that what the Logos is (God) and what he comes to be (man) is not changed or confused in the 'becoming' but rather the 'becoming' maintains the fact that the Logos remains God and establishes the fact that the Logos comes to be and is truly and fully man.[4]

Nevertheless, the fundamental Christological issue had, Weinandy tells us, already been grasped by Cyril:

> Cyril realizes that for a true understanding of the Incarnation the 'becoming' must be such that it not only allows for the fact that God *is* man, that Christ, as one ontological being, is God incarnate; but he also realizes that for a true understanding of the Incarnation the 'becoming' must be such

that God remains God in the 'becoming' if it is *God* who is man, and likewise the manhood must remain unchanged if it is *man* that God has become. Patristic Christological development has finally reached the ultimate question in Cyril. How does one conceive of such a notion of 'become', a notion of 'become' that guarantees that the Logos *is* man, that it is the *Logos* who is man, and that it is *man* that the Logos is? Has Cyril conceived 'become' in such a way that such a union is effected?[5]

Weinandy's answer to this question is that Cyril at least wishes to understand 'become' and the union in this way, but that he does not fully explicate the necessary notion. And in all the subsequent discussion Weinandy asks of each of the Christologies that he investigates whether it gives an affirmative answer to this threefold 'ultimate question'.

For reasons of space he passes over the later development of Greek Christology and, with a brief but relevant examination of Anselm, he deals in some detail with St Thomas Aquinas. Having expounded St Thomas's doctrine of the divine immutability on the basis of the Thomist understanding of God as *ipsum esse*, self-existent being, Weinandy quotes St Thomas to the effect that 'the mystery of the Incarnation was not completed through God being changed in any way from the immutable state in which he had been from all eternity, but through his having united himself to the creature in a new way or rather through having united it to himself.'[6] This he expands as follows:

It is not by chance that Aquinas emphasizes that the human nature 'is united to' or 'accrued to' the Logos. The incarnational act is not one of local motion or change on the part of the Logos, as if he somehow 'left heaven' and 'came down' to earth, and changed himself into man. Rather the incarnational act, the 'becoming' is the uniting of a human nature to the very person of the Logos in such a way that the Logos exists as man. This union with the Logos then is not by way of some mediating act on the part of the Logos, but rather the human nature is united to the very person of the Logos as the Logos *is*, as he exists immutably as God, in his *esse personale*. The Logos acquires no new personal being, as Aquinas states (if he did, he would no longer be God); but rather he (as God) acquires a new mode of existing (as man), and this can be accomplished only if the human nature is united to him as he really is in his *esse personale* as God. Aquinas' use of the term *'esse personale'* specifies that the union is in the Logos as he is as God, and thus does not change, thus assuring not only the immutability of God for God's sake, but also for the sake of the Incarnation, that is, so that it is really the Logos *as God* who becomes and is man. In so doing Aquinas likewise guarantees that the Logos *is* man and exists *as man*. Since the human nature is united to the very person of the Logos, the Logos must subsist in it and thus truly *be man*. . . .

While it may seem paradoxical, but nevertheless true, what Aquinas is pointing out is that the union must be in the person of the Logos if it is to be really the *Logos* who is man, and thus the 'becoming' must be the uniting of the human nature to the very person of the Logos as he exists as God if it is *to be really man* that the Logos becomes.[7]

Thus it is clear that Godhead undergoes neither diminution nor augmentation nor modification in itself by the fact that the person of the Logos becomes the subject of a human nature; in this sense the divine immutability is preserved. But, it may be asked, and St Thomas recognizes this, does not the addition of the human nature imply, in itself, a kind of change in the Logos who has really and not fictitiously become its subject?

St Thomas's reply to this objection is surprising and it might seem at first sight to suggest that God has not really become man after all. 'This union', he writes, 'is not really in God, but in our way of thinking, for God is said to be united to a creature inasmuch as the creature is really united to God without any change in him.'[8] As Weinandy says:

In placing the incarnational act within the conceptual framework of relations, Aquinas has made an original contribution to Christology. However, on first reading the above, it seems to raise more questions that it answers. The obvious initial reaction is that such a relation is no relation at all. God may appear to be related, but really is not. It only seems so to our way of thinking. For this reason a short study of Aquinas' understanding of relations must be made before trying to explicate exactly what Aquinas is trying to say about the incarnational act as relational.[9]

And in making this examination Weinandy himself makes an important and original amplification, or indeed correction, of Aquinas.

> Relation by definition involves two extremes, terms or subjects. Now the relation between two subjects can be logical or real, and it can be logical or real in three ways. Both terms can be logically related, really related, or the relation can be logical in one term and real in the other. This last can be called a mixed relation. . . . When two terms are related logically, nothing in the reality of the terms undergoes change since the relation is made in the mind. To say that Fido is related to the canine species does not change Fido or the canine species. . . . Real relations are the most commonly considered and experienced. The relation is due to something in the reality of the terms themselves and what establishes the relation is due to something they have in common or brings about some change in the terms due to some causality. One person is relatively taller than another for both have height in common. A brother and sister are related because they have the same parents in common. A man is not a father until he has a son.[10]

The third kind of relation involves a change in one of the terms but not in the other. One of the stock examples is that of knowledge. If I come to know the height of Mount Everest, this brings about a change in me, for it adds to my store of information, but it does not bring about a change in the height of Everest, which remains what it was before. Now St Thomas takes as typical mixed relations that of creation, which, he says, brings about a change in the creature but none in the Creator, and that of the incarnation, which brings about a change in Christ's human nature but none in the person of the Word; and he remarks that in such a relation the two terms are not in the same order of being. However, one of his favourite clarificatory illustrations is that of a man moving from the right to the left of a column, which, he says makes a change in the man, since right and left are due to the man's conceptual understanding of place (as we might say, he carries his co-ordinate system with him) but in no way affects the column. However, Weinandy points out, right and left have nothing to do with the terms being in different orders of being and St

Thomas's illustration is thoroughly misleading:

> Aquinas gives the impression that to be a logical term in a
> mixed relation means there is no relation in the real term
> other than that man's mind so conceives it to be. Man's mind
> brings the relation about. *In reality* the logical term has no
> relation to the real term at all. If that were the case God
> would not in reality be the creator, man in reality would not
> be a knower,[11] and the Logos in reality would not be man,
> but only so conceived to be in man's mind.[12]

'However', he adds,

> it would seem that Aquinas does not mean that. In a true
> mixed relation the logical term is in a radically different
> situation as will be seen. Nevertheless, this ambiguity will
> keep appearing in Aquinas' treatment of mixed relations.[13]

In order to straighten out St Thomas's doctrine of mixed
relations and its application to the incarnation, Weinandy first
considers the logically prior question of creation:

> To create demands that God acts by no other act than by the
> act that he is as *ipsum esse* for no other act will do.
> But . . . then obviously creation does not change or affect
> God. The whole effect is in the creature precisely because it is
> in being related to God as *ipsum esse* that he comes to be.
> That God is only logically related to creatures is not
> something negative, but rather specifies and clarifies the
> exact nature of the real relation in creatures; that is, a
> relatedness to God as he is in himself as *ipsum esse* which
> affects the very coming to be and continued existence of the
> creature. . . .
> For God to be the logical term of the relationship does not
> mean that he is not closely related to the creature. Just
> as . . . to say that creation does not mean change does not
> imply a lack of dynamism, but rather something more
> dynamic than any change or movement could be, so now to
> say that God is logically related to creatures demands a
> closeness to creatures which is far greater than any mutually
> real relation. . . . God is present in the creature by his very
> essence, by the pure act that he is. . . . Even pantheism falls
> short of such a close relationship.[14]

Weinandy now stresses the importance of the fact that the two terms of the relation are in distinct ontological orders:

> The relation is real in that [sc. the lesser] term precisely in that the term comes to be and exists. It is logical in the other term because the second term is totally dependent for its existence on being related to the first term *as the first is in itself*, and not by any other act. Thus one sees that to describe a relation as logical in one term and real in the other is to predicate a creative relationship, and one then that is supremely dynamic and intimate. [15]

In true Thomist fashion Weinandy gets St Thomas out of a difficulty by making a new and highly important distinction:

> God for Aquinas *is* in reality creator, but he is creator not because of a newness within his being, but because *in reality* something is newly related to him as he is, the creature. It is because the creature is really related to God as the source of its being, that God is actually related to him as creator. Thus one can say that while God is the logical term of a mixed relation in that he does not change, nor establishes the relation by some mediating act, but by relating the creature to himself as he is, he nevertheless is actually related to the creature because the creature is really related to him. [16]

This last sentence contains the heart of the matter. Weinandy convicts the Angelic Doctor, not of holding a false doctrine of creation, but of an ambiguous use of the word 'logical' which obscures the expression of the truth which he holds:

> He never explicitly distinguishes the difference between being a 'logical term' in a mutual logical relation and being a 'logical term' in a mixed relation. . . . In a true mixed relation, the logical term is related not because man establishes the relation in his mind, but to the fact that *in reality* some second term is really related to it as it is in itself and not by any mediating action, and thus *in reality* the logical term is actually related. . . . While in both instances the logical term remains unchanged (and this is why Aquinas uses the term in both instances), yet in a mixed relation a further note is added to the concept of 'logical term', that of *actually* being related to the second term because the second term is really related to it. [17]

I am not convinced that Weinandy has been very happy in his adoption of the word 'actual' in this context, but I confess that I have not thought of a better one. Nor, as Weinandy remarks, had St Thomas, nor has anyone since. And 'real relations are obviously actual also.'[18] The concept itself is of central importance, as we shall see when we go on to consider its relevance to the incarnation.

In many respects, as Weinandy points out, the relations of creation and incarnation are analogous. Both are mixed relations, and in Weinandy's sense, 'actual'. Each has an uncreated and a created term, and in each the two terms are directly related without any intermediate factor:

> By maintaining that the Logos is the logical term of the relation, and this is the main point, Aquinas specifies the closeness and depth of the real effect in the humanity. The grace of the union or the created relational effect in the humanity is not 'ordained to (another) act, but to the personal being [*ad esse personale*] of the Logos' [*S. Th*. III, viii, 5 *ad* 3). . . . This makes it possible to maintain that it is really the Logos *as God* who is man. . . . Because the Logos as the logical term remains unchanged, and thus in turn making it possible for the real effect in the humanity to be that of coming to be and being united to the Logos as he is, one can grasp how in the Incarnation it can really be *God* who is man, and truly *man* that God is. All this can be said briefly by stating that the real created effect in the humanity is nothing other than the eternal uncreated Logos subsisting in it. . . .
>
> The Logos is understood to be related, and actually is related, not by some effect or change in him, but because the manhood is really related to him.[19]

What Weinandy does not explicitly point out here, though he undoubtedly assumes it and it is basic to his entire position, is the precise *difference* between the relations of creation and incarnation. This is that creation establishes the finite term, the creature, as a subsistent entity, with its own substantial *esse* though in complete dependence upon the creator, while in incarnation the finite term, the human nature of Christ, subsists only in the *esse personale* of the Logos. This is, as indeed Weinandy recognizes, the basis of the concept of the 'communication of idioms': 'It is because one and the same person *is* both God and man that one can truly predicate to each the attributes of the other. . . . The attributes are not then predicated directly to each nature, but to the person who exists both as God and as man.'[20] But, having briefly sketched this notion, he significantly resumes his theme as follows:

> What must be pointed out concerning Aquinas is not so much the above, but rather the incarnational relevance of the immutability of God to his passibility as man. . . .
>
> Aquinas in his Christology was motivated to uphold the immutability of the Logos not just for *theo*-logical reasons, but primarily for incarnational reasons. The Logos for Aquinas must remain immutable in becoming man, not only because he is God, but also to ensure the fact that it is truly *God* who *is man*. The same incarnational motivation is present in Aquinas' treatment of the *passibility of God* as man. . . .
>
> While Aquinas does not say it explicitly, what is present in his incarnational motivation for the immutability of God is the paradox that God must remain immutable in becoming man so that it is truly God who is mutable and passible as man.[21]

This last sentence is of prime importance, for it is widely believed that to insist on the impassibility and immutability of the Godhead is to deny that God is genuinely concerned with the affairs of man and to give him at most the status of a detached observer. The words in which Weinandy sums up his examination of St Thomas stress the falsity of any such assumption:

> While much of the above treatment of Aquinas may seem abstract and 'lifeless' it is here where all that went before gains in meaning. Every human being thirsts, hungers, suffers, dies, and for Christ to be just another man added to the human race makes little difference. It is only if Christ is truly God who as man thirsts, hungers, suffers, dies, in time and history that time and history and every human life is changed and made new.[22]

I shall discuss the remainder of Dr Weinandy's thesis in much less detail, as it is in his examination of the Angelic Doctor that he has made his most important and original contribution to Christology. The rest of his work consists of a systematic application of the insights there acquired to the teaching of later writers. Maintaining his methodological principle that the heart of any Christology lies in its understanding of the term 'become' in the formula 'God becomes man', he proceeds to his final discussion of contemporary Catholic Christology by way of two chapters devoted to Kenotic Christology and Process-Christology respectively.

Kenotic Christology he sees as dominated by the notion of 'become' as *compositional*. For Luther, whom he sees as the herald of kenoticism, 'the Incarnation takes place because of a union of natures forming the divine/human reality of Christ. The "becoming" is once more compositional, the coming together of natures, rather than existential and personal, the coming to be, the coming to exist of the person of the Logos as man. . . . For Luther the existential reality of Jesus is God as God in a substantial and dynamic union with a man as man, but God never *is* man nor does he exist *as man*.'[23] The kenoticists whom Weinandy takes most seriously are the Anglicans Charles Gore and Frank Weston, for both of whom the central problem was that of the limited, or even erroneous, character of Christ's human knowledge. Both of these thinkers were insistent that the person of Jesus was God the eternal Word, but this demanded a self-limitation (Gore) or at least a self-restraint (Weston) of the Word within the sphere of the human life. In Weinandy's words:

> Some sort of change is demanded. While most kenoticists, and this is especially evident in Gore and Weston, want it to be God the Logos who is man, they nevertheless feel that it cannot be the Logos as he fully exists as God without destroying the manhood. The Logos in some manner has to gear himself down to a human level if he is to become man.[24]

However:

> As soon as one sees the incarnational act, the 'becoming', not as the substantial compositional union of natures forming a new being, but as the person of the Logos taking on a new manner or mode of existence, of *coming to be, coming to exist* as man, the question and problem as asked and un-

derstood by the kenoticists disappears. The 'becoming' no longer threatens the immutable divinity of the Logos, nor the integrity of the manhood; but just the opposite. It establishes and guarantees that it is the Logos, in his *unqualified* divinity, who now is and exists *as man*. Thus *as man* the Logos, without any change in his divine nature, possesses a human intellect and will, and thus human consciousness and knowledge.[25]

There is, moreover, a further defect which Weinandy discerns in the English kenoticists, though it was absent from Luther; this was their definition of personhood as psychological self-consciousness. The consequence was that they were faced with the alternatives of either seeing the Logos as losing his divine self-consciousness in order to retain the unity of his person or else as becoming in effect two persons in order to have both a divine and a human self-consciousness:

What one ends up with in the Kenotic Christ is not a real human consciousness or knowledge, nor a real humanity, but rather an adapted *divine* consciousness and knowledge tailored to a human level.[26]

Weinandy's final verdict is that, in their concentration upon Christ's consciousness and knowledge the kenoticists can be said to be the first modern Christologists. But, he adds tellingly, 'whether contemporary theologians have learned from their mistakes and have given up their false presuppositions and notions is another question.'[27]

Passing to the process-theologians, for whom he describes 'becoming' as *prehension* (the term derives, of course, from A. N. Whitehead), Weinandy remarks that in the setting of their thought the basic Christological questions simply do not arise. Since it is their fundamental postulate that God is mutable and that his nature is one of change, the question how he can remain immutable in becoming man and be passible as man is just a non-question. Thus, although he selects for detailed exposition the Christology of the three typical writers W. Norman Pittenger, David Griffin, and Schubert Ogden, Weinandy's critique is directed mainly to their fundamental doctrine of God and his relation to creation. 'The presence of God in Jesus may be to such a degree that it highlights in what way he is present in every other occasion, but it is metaphysically impossible for him to be present in an altogether new way.'[28] The basic philosophical defect of process-theology is its inability to account for the existence of anything: 'It is impossible for God to give "being" since his being as an actual concrete reality is totally dependent on the world; and thus, if anything, the world exists chronologically and logically prior to God.'[29] Nor, in spite of its claims, is this notion of God really dynamic:

> While God is always changing, it does not imply any dynamic action in the world on his part, but the lack of action since every change in him is one of actualizing some potential *within himself*. . . .
>   He acts as the divine lure or influence on reality. . . . However, one should not think that this is God acting in some dynamic way, or for that matter that it is God acting at all. . . . His lure and influence is not a dynamic action on his part, but the mere presence of his pure potential, that 'part' of him which is undynamic, unactualized, and non-existent.[30]

Furthermore—and this is the greatest weakness of process-philosophy—if it is true, no two fully constituted and actual entities, no two persons for example, can ever be literally related to each other, or to anything else at all:

> Thus to speak of God suffering with man or sharing man's joys is at best a euphemism. All that means is that God records in his present consequent nature that a man suffer*ed* or that a man *was* happy, but when God prehends it, it is not present to him as the contemporary pain or joy of a man. It is merely the objective past idea. God then literally *lives* in the past.[31]

Weinandy finally has no difficulty in showing that process-philosophy is simply incapable of meeting the demands that Christianity makes upon Christology. Like traditional thought, it desires to maintain that God is supremely dynamic and is intimately related to the world and man, and that in the incarnation God really does become man and act as man in time and history. But it completely fails in its attempt.[32]

In his final chapter Weinandy examines the writings of three contemporary Christologists under the rubric ' ''Become'' as dynamically present.' All three—Piet Schoonenberg, Karl Rahner, and Jean Galot—I have commented upon at lesser or greater length in my recent book *Theology and the Gospel of Christ*, and the last of them in considerable detail. Weinandy's assessments seem to me to be thoroughly accurate and to show great insight.

Schoonenberg's guiding principle, as expounded and applied in his book *The Christ*,[33] is that, while the world and man are dependent upon God for their being, God never intervenes in the world in any way. For him, the notion that God is the primary efficient cause and man the secondary efficient cause of human acts, in such a way that man's freedom is not destroyed by God but rather established by him, is incoherent and impossible: 'for God to act in a radically different way in time and history other than through the normal created laws of nature and evolution or through the free decisions of men would of necessity make God an unbecoming intruder and competitor of man.'[34] Thus Schoonenberg cannot hold that the person of Christ is the pre-existent Logos and can claim to be in line with Chalcedon only by interpreting Chalcedon as teaching that the historical person and reality of Jesus is the result of the union of the two natures.[35] Indeed he goes further and asserts that 'Jesus Christ is one person. He is a human person',[36] and even that 'it is primarily not the human nature which is enhypostatic in the divine person, but the divine nature in the human person', so that the Word 'is divine person through being a human person.'[37] But, as Weinandy points out, Schoonenberg's whole criticism against Christ being the pre-existent Logos rests on the false supposition that, if God acts in time and history in new ways in and through man, he must denigrate man: 'Schoonenberg, as many before him, has not grasped the fact that for the person of the Logos to become man is for the Logos *to be man*, and precisely because of this it really and truly is *man* that the Logos is. Nothing in the man Jesus is eliminated, superseded, or lost. What is affirmed is only that who it is who is this man is the Logos.'[38]

Karl Rahner, whose Christology is to be gathered from various volumes of his *Theological Investigations*,[39] stands in many ways at the opposite pole from Schoonenberg. For him, far from man's genuine reality opposing a barrier to God's intervention, the essence of human nature is its capacity to receive and express God's revelation of himself. If God has really become man, 'the presupposition is that man is what comes to be when God wishes to reveal and express himself as he is in himself in time and history.'[40] There is therefore no problem in God becoming man while remaining God. Furthermore—and Rahner is emphatic on this—since it is not just *God* who becomes man, but *God the Word*, there must be a special affinity between manhood and the Second Person of the Trinity. Rahner explicitly rejects St Thomas's view that any one of the three Persons might have become incarnate; he holds that only the Son could be the subject of a human nature, while holding that the Father and the Spirit are also involved in the incarnation each in his appropriate way.[41]

Weinandy firmly commends Rahner's position about the diversity of Christ's natures in relation to the incarnational act:

> The distinction of natures or modes of existence must not be made prior to the union (either temporally or logically), for any subsequent ontological union would destroy either or both the humanity or divinity. Rather the distinction must be made within the one reality of Christ precisely because the very act which establishes the ontological oneness is the same act which establishes and guarantees the distinction.[42]

He finds some difficulty, however, in Rahner's famous formula, which its author himself describes as 'dialectical', that, 'while God remains immutable "in himself", he can come to be "in the other", and that *both* assertions must really and truly be made of the same God as God.'[43] Nevertheless, in opposition to Schoonenberg, Donceel, and Trethowan, Weinandy, while admitting in Rahner some confusion of expression, does not take him as meaning that the Logos changes in becoming man or that God in his divinity undergoes change:

> All of this complexity, confusion, and misunderstanding could easily be eliminated if Rahner had realized that God's actual existence as man is not dialectically opposed to his immutability and his being a logical term in the incarnational relation. . . . God himself as he is in himself can actually become man in reality without change, not in spite

of his immutability, but precisely because of it. Because he is immutable he is able to relate the manhood to himself *as he is* so as to subsist in it and be man.[44]

The third contemporary Christologist whom Weinandy discusses, Père Jean Galot, as he says 'is not a very well known theologian in English-speaking circles, and one wonders if he is appreciated even on the Continent.' Nevertheless his estimate that '[Galot's] Christology and soteriology is one of the most refreshing and clearly rendered statements of the Catholic tradition' and that it 'is not just a restatement of the past, but an attempt to truly develop the untapped potential of traditional belief'[45] is, in my judgement, fully justified, and it was for this reason that I devoted nearly forty tightly packed pages to discussing it in my book *Theology and the Gospel of Christ*.[46] (I might add that it was in conversation with Fr Weinandy as his supervisor that I first came to know of Galot's work.) Weinandy's discussion is much shorter than mine, but we agree in applauding Galot for his development of the inherent, but hitherto latent, dynamism of the Chalcedonian definition. But we both identify a weakness at one particular point.[47] Weinandy makes the point by saying that 'Galot, like Rahner, confuses the question of the Logos changing *in becoming man* with the question of the Logos *changing as man*, and thus comes up with a somewhat ambiguous answer.'[48] 'Because the effect of the "becoming" places the Logos in a situation where as man he is the subject of change Galot tends to see the "becoming" itself, the act by which the Logos comes to be the subject of change, as bringing about a change in the Logos' divinity as well.'[49] Thus, without formally denying God's immutability, Galot sees God as using his immutable power in different ways at different times in what might be called 'sequential mutations'. 'He sequentially changes himself into God *the Creator* and God who *has become man*.'[50] Galot feels he must propose that because God is immutable he can change his *in se* immutability into a *pro me* immutability',[51] but this is nevertheless a *change*. However, Weinandy says, this is quite unnecessary:

> Once one realizes that God is actually Creator because creatures in reality are really related to him as such, then God as God (*in se*) and God as Creator (*pro me*) are one and the

same. Likewise, the Logos is actually man *as he is in himself as God* because the humanity in reality is related to him as he is in such a way that the Logos *in se* subsists as man *pro me*. For God to be logically related guarantees, specifies and establishes that it is God himself as he is in himself who is actually related to man and actually is man. [52]

And Weinandy suggests that his differences are at least to some extent verbal by immediately adding 'This is ultimately what Galot wishes to say and maintain all along.' (It is of course important to remember the specialized sense that Weinandy gives to the word 'actual' in his discussion of mixed relations. [53]) He also remarks that Galot's argument, which is set out in his book *Vers une nouvelle christologie*, [54] would have been very much strengthened and its defects avoided if he had incorporated into it the original and illuminating under-standing of divine and human personality (person as relational being) which is manifested in his earlier work *La Personne du Christ*. [55] In spite of this one criticism Weinandy has no hesitation in stressing that 'Galot's Christology is one of the most theologically exciting to appear in recent years' [56] and it is significant that it is at the end of his discussion of Galot that he most naturally summarizes his own position:

Where in man the person is relational through and in his nature which is distinct from his personhood, the persons of the Trinity are identical with the one nature of God. Thus while a human person is in potency to become further relational, divine persons are fully relational, fully actualized relations, fully personal, since they relationally are the immutable and fully actualized nature of God as *actus purus*. Human persons, then, unlike divine persons, change in every new relation. The relations they establish are through changes in their natures through and in which they relate to others. . . .

However, the divine persons, being fully actualized relations, are related to one another *as they are*, and not by mediating actions. They actually come to be in their very relatedness and are their relatedness. Because of this when God in the Trinity of Persons establishes relations outside himself, he is able to do so not by mediating acts which involve change, but by relating the other person to himself as he is. The Persons of the Trinity being fully actualized relations contain no potency [i.e. no *potentiality*] which needs to be actualized or overcome through new actions in order to establish new relations. What needs to be changed and overcome is man's potential to be related. This is done by God relating man to himself as he is in different ways. No intermediating action then lies between or establishes the relation between God and the other. . . .

The same is the case in the Incarnation. The Logos being a fully actualized subsistent relation does not have to overcome some potential in order to become man and subsist as man. He does not . . . have to change his immutable being or newly express it as incarnational. The Logos being a fully actualized subsistent relation has no relational potency and thus has no need of new mediating actions on his part in order for him to establish an incarnational relation. The potency lies solely in the humanity. It must be related and united to the Logos in such a way that the effect in the humanity is nothing other than the Logos subsisting in it as man. . . .

The immutability of God as expressed in the person of the Logos as a fully actualized subsistent relation is the prolegomenon to and presupposition for the Incarnation and not a stumbling block.[57]

SOME FURTHER CONSIDERATIONS

As one looks back on Dr Weinandy's argument it is, in my judgement, clear that he has made two contributions of major importance to contemporary Christology. The first is to have made it explicit that, when it is God who is the subject of becoming, *becoming* does not involve *change*; this is what in his discussion of Chalcedon he denotes by the phrase ' "become" as personal/existential' and which, if correctly applied, he sees as not incompatible with the modern demand for ' "become" as dynamically present'. His second contribution—and it is closely linked with the first—is his amplification and development of the Thomist doctrine of 'mixed relations', with his recognition that, when the 'logical term' of a mixed relation is God, we have a special case which must be treated as such and is not to be casually passed over by super-

ficial and univocal generalities. What I have now to say will
largely consist of some further filling out of these insights, but I
must make it plain that, in spite of my indebtedness to Dr
Weinandy for them, I cannot hold him responsible for the use
which I shall have made of them.

First of all, I would stress that the relation between an uncreated and a created term, described by Weinandy as an *actual*
mixed relation is thoroughly concrete at both its *uncreated and
its created end*. The technical description of it as 'logical and
not real in the uncreated term' is valid as indicating that God
does not *change* as a result of the establishment of the relation,
but it would be misleading if it were taken as meaning that the
relation is merely fictitious in God. It is right to reject the claim
that the establishment of the relation must bring about a
change in God on the alleged ground that before its establishment he was not its subject but after its establishment
he was; but this rejection depends not upon its attribution to
him being fictitious but upon the fact that he is not in time in
any case, so that the use of the words 'before' and 'after' in this
context is improper, and upon the further fact, about which I
shall have more to say later on,[1] that he is infinite.

Secondly, and closely connected with this, is the fact that the
doctrine of relation with which we are concerned is a matter of
metaphysics and not just of logic and linguistics, though its
pursuit does of course involve the use both of reason and of
speech. Just as, in the doctrine of analogy, we are, as I have
argued elsewhere, 'not merely concerned with the question
"How can an infinite, necessary and immutable Being be
described in terms that are derived from the finite, contingent
and mutable world?" but with a question that is anterior to this
and without which this cannot be properly discussed at all,
namely "How is the possibility of our applying to the infinite
Being terms that are derived from the finite order conditioned
by the fact that the finite order is dependent for its very
existence on the fiat of the infinite and self-existent
Being?"',[2] so here too I would urge that we shall accept the
notion of the actual mixed relation as intelligible only if we
have a thorough grasp of the concrete character of its terms and
of the dependence of the created term upon the uncreated.
Without this, I am pretty sure, the notion itself, and the
correlative notion of *becoming that does not involve change*,

will appear to be logically incoherent and self-contradictory. I do not mean to suggest that reality itself is self-contradictory or irrational, but rather that its richness is such as to overflow the limits of any linguistic structures or conceptual systems that are merely linguistically based. This is true, I believe, even of the natural world; to quote myself again, 'So far from consisting of atomic facts which can be put in one-to-one correspondence with atomic linguistic statements, the world (at least as it appears to us) is a continuous, multidimensional, dynamic entity, while language is discrete, undimensional and static.'[3] And if this is true of the natural world considered in abstraction from its relation to its transcendent Creator, it can hardly be false or irrelevant when we are concerned with its relation to him. There are various cases in which Christian truths have broken through the bonds of Aristotelian logic, to the apparent destruction but the ultimate enrichment of the latter—the doctrine of the Trinity is one, the doctrine of human survival of bodily death is another—and this may provide a further example.

Thirdly, the actual mixed relation (which I will henceforth denote as AMR) can hold only between an uncreated and a created term. It is only because the first term is altogether self-existent and the second term altogether dependent upon the first that the first term can be in actual relation to the second without undergoing change as a result of the relation. And in fact the primary example of an AMR is the relation of creation itself and it is presupposed by all other AMRs. (It is significant that Weinandy, although he was explicitly concerned with the incarnation, found it necessary to discuss creation first.)[4] For it is of the essence of an AMR that it unites two terms, one of which owes both its existence and its place in the relation to the other, while the other owes nothing whatever to the one.

Fourthly—and this is largely but not entirely a verbal matter—there is an ambiguity in the notion of relation itself, which is harmless provided it is recognized and whose recognition is itself illuminating. The classical starting-point for a discussion of relations is Aristotle's *Categories*, concerning which the two leading authorities have remarked that it 'is a work of exceptional ambiguity both in purpose and content', the two major ambiguities being that 'it is unclear whether Aristotle is classifying symbols or what they symbolize' and that 'it is not clear whether Aristotle is concerned with predicates only or with terms in general, including subjects.'[5] It is not, however, with these particular ambiguities that I am here concerned, and, whether or not Aristotle himself was clear about the distinction, we may, I hope, agree that the doctrine must be about both symbols and what they symbolize, about both words and things, and that it is about words only because it is about things in the first place, because, as I have already urged, logic and linguistics need to be based in metaphysics. The ambiguity to which I wish to point is of a different type.

In its linguistic or logical aspect, *relation* is, for Aristotle, one of the ten 'categories' or, in the scholastic rendering, 'predicaments',[6] that is to say, the ten modes in which a term can be predicated of a subject. These are listed as substance, quantity, quality, relation, place, time, position, habitus, action, and passion; and, without pausing to argue the adequacy of this classification or to determine the precise meaning of each word, we must notice two points. (1) Substance has a status different from, and prior to, all the other categories. It cannot be predicated of any other category, but other categories are predicated of it. Passing from the logical to the real aspect, this means that substances are not inherent in attributes but attributes are inherent in them. In other words, all the other nine categories are 'accidental'; only substance is 'substantial'. (2) Nevertheless, relation stands out from the rest of the nine accidental categories in that, while it is predicated of a subject, it involves another term as well. To say that John is ugly involves nobody but John, but to say that John is uglier than Paul, although it is a statement about John and not about Paul, brings Paul into the picture as well. It is this special characteristic of the category of relation that was so skilfully made use of by St Augustine in his exposition of the doctrine of the Trinity[7] and that has in our own time been turned to such good account by Père Jean Galot in Christology;[8] this is not, however, our immediate concern. What I wish to point out is that, because this traditional approach still sees relation as one of the categories, albeit as a category of a unique kind, it still tends to view it as attributing a predicate to a single subject, in spite of the fact that a second term is involved within the predicate. To use a simple symbolism and denoting the fact that a has the relation R to b by the formula $a\mathrm{R}b$, we are still thinking of *a* as *having-the-relation-R-to-b* rather than thinking of *a* and *b* as having their several roles within the common relation R; thinking of *a*–(R*b*) rather than of R(*ab*). Now I do not want to suggest that it is false to assert *a*–(R*b*) or the converse *b*–(R̄*a*), so long as these are seen as consequences of the wider scope of R(*ab*), of the two terms in their common relatedness.[9] Nor do I suggest that, in itself, the formula either implies or excludes that the two terms are on the same metaphysical level; this will depend on the circumstances of each particular case. And I think it will be most useful to keep this distinction in mind in reflecting on such AMRs as divine prevenience in human acts, the incarnation and grace, for in each case the created term of the relation owes its very existence to the uncreated term. And here I am perhaps going beyond Weinandy's own expressed position in affirming that, while the totally asymmetric character of the creator/creature relation altogether rules out any change in God, nevertheless the creator is genuinely involved in the creature's existence and vicissitudes.

As the title of his thesis announces, Weinandy's purpose was to demonstrate that the assumption of a real and complete human nature by the Person of God the Son did not impair his divine immutability and impassibility; it provided the impassible God with a nature in which he could really and not just fictitiously suffer. In the patristic phrase, 'one of the Holy Trinity suffered in the flesh', for 'we needed a God made flesh and put to death in order that we could live again.'[10] In the human nature of Christ *and only in the human nature of Christ* does one of the Persons of the Godhead become the actual subject of a human life and undergo human vicissitudes and experience human joys and sorrows. Only of the Second Person, and only of him in his manhood, can we say *passus, crucifixus, mortuus et sepultus*. Nevertheless, the question can still be asked whether God's personal involvement with man's existence, and in particular with man's sufferings, is confined within the human nature of God the Son. Is all that is said in Scripture and in Christian literature down the ages about the love, the yearning, the compassion of the Father or, to take but one instance, St Paul's phrase about the unutterable groanings of the Spirit,[11] to be taken as pure metaphor and as nothing more than the attribution to God of emotions which we experience in ourselves? To ask such questions one does not have to be a process-theologian or a believer in a finite God, or to hold with A. N. Whitehead that 'God is the great companion—the fellow-sufferer who understands.'[12] We need only recall that the most traditional theology has spoken not only of the impassibility but also of the compassion of God, even if it has tended to stress the former more than the latter and to treat the divine compassion as the sphere of the preacher and the devotional writer rather than of the dogmatic theologian. Professor H. P. Owen has described the impassibility of God as 'the most questionable aspect of classical theism',[13] but in the brief space which he devotes to the topic he suggests three considerations which may make the impassibility and the compassion of God more obviously reconcilable: (1) 'the sorrow and pain that God experiences are wholly vicarious; they consist entirely in his imaginative response to the sin and suffering that afflict his creatures'; (2) 'any suffering that God endures through his love for his creatures is immediately transfigured by the joy that is necessarily his within his uncreated Godhead'; (3) 'there are analogies even in human experience to the transfiguration of God's sorrow in his joy.'[14] In the six-volume encyclopaedia *Sacramentum Mundi*,[15] Walter Kern writes, in his article 'God-World Relationship':

> As regards a real relationship appertaining in itself to the order of reality, between God and the world, i.e., relating God to the world, philosophy—and traditional theology for the most part—hold that this must be denied. Today, however, theological reflection is inclined to maintain the reality of the relationship, of God, the God of grace, to man and the world.[16]

He goes on to state the position (*a*) in philosophy and (*b*) in theology, before (*c*) giving his own 'middle position', which he describes as 'necessarily very fluid and open'.

> The philosophical reasons against a real relationship [writes Kern] aim at preserving God's absolute independence as regards all that is not God, and the immutability thereby involved. A relationship to the world would change God, because it would add something real to his being, like an accident. . . . A real relationship of God to the world would

be dependent on the reality of the world as the necessary condition of the relationship. Hence God would not be the Infinite Absolute, utterly independent of all that is not God.[17]

This is, of course, the established position, but Kern sees its stringency as questionable. It would hold, he says,

> only if the world, as fundament and presupposition of the relation, were a real factor in the setting-up of the relationship (which would then be conceived as static). But [he asks] would God be conditioned by and dependent on the world if his creative will, the free decision whereby he really and effectively wills from eternity that the world should be in time, is so purely dynamically and purposefully referred to the world that the world is, of itself, only consecutive to, and not constitutive of, the real relationship of God to the world? . . . [So, he concludes] God in himself does not become different by this willed act (even if we suppose that it contains a real relationship to the world—which is the question).[18]

In contrast to this 'philosophical' view, Kern now places 'the theological affirmation of the ''reality of the relation of God to his creatures''' as 'now based principally on the personal character of the encounter between man and the Creator-God of free grace'.

The dogma of grace means real 'intersubjectivity' between God and man, a

> living fellowship of love, not two 'one-way streets', but a common current to and fro. That the relational can exist, without being relative in the sense of the imperfect, is attested by the revelation of the Trinity in God.[19]

It is stressed that, on the one hand, 'the supposition of a real relationship to the world may not [i.e. must not] affect the absolute independence of God', while, on the other hand, 'the immutability of God must not be confused with frozen rigidity', and, indeed, 'the mystery of the way God is immutable surpasses human understanding.'[20]

Kern's own position is not altogether easy to understand. He asserts that 'God changes because he becomes man. . . . But

God, the Absolute, Infinite and Simple, cannot change intrinsically. Hence he changes, not in himself, but in something else belonging to himself.'[21] At first sight, this might seem to restrict God's 'change' simply to his becoming incarnate, but later statements make it plain that it refers to his creation of the world as well. 'God, the "self-determining subsistent", determines himself to becoming man and to creating the world, and becomes and is creator and man: he himself, in the otherness of himself, bringing this other continually to be, through himself, through the subsistent freedom which is his being.'[22] But, apart from this passing reference to 'subsistent freedom' and a repudiation of any 'comprehensible—that is, Hegelian—synthesis', Kern throws no further light upon this mystery.

A very similar attitude is shown in the anonymous article 'Impassibility of God' in *The Oxford Dictionary of the Christian Church*.[23] Immutability and all-sufficiency in God are seen as being philosophical and Greek, love and sympathy as religious and Hebrew, and the conclusion is that 'perhaps . . . truth lies in the recognition that both aspects must be preserved in a way that it is beyond the competence of human reason to exhibit.' The most helpful discussion which I have seen, however, is that contained in Père Jean Galot's book *Dieu souffre-t-il?*;[24] it confirms the opinion which I have expressed elsewhere of the author as 'the most constructively creative, and also one of the most judicious, of living Christologists',[25] though it extends beyond the strictly Christological realm.

BEING AND LOVE: FR GALOT'S APPROACH

Galot explicitly approaches his problem 'not from the philosophical point of view of the abstract possibility of pain in God but from the positive indications of Revelation: in the concrete visage of the God who reveals himself do we discover certain elements of pain and how must they be understood?'[1] And the primary fact is that 'at the centre of Revelation we find not a demonstration of the impassible presence of God but the Passion of the Son of God incarnate.'[2] In the theology of the early centuries he finds as specially suggestive the formulas 'God has suffered' and 'One of the Trinity has suffered', scandalous as these, and especially the latter, have seemed to many. He insists on their metaphysical concreteness, while admitting their linguistic and logical aspects:

> It was not grammatical links or logical relations that introduced the principle of the *communicatio idiomatum* and in particular the affirmation that God suffered. The principle rests on the ontological constitution of Christ, and more precisely on the unity of his person; its value is essentially ontological. It signifies that the divine person of the Word is really involved in suffering.[3]

The orthodox fathers, especially the Greeks, were quite clear about this, though the medievals 'passed it by in silence or simply failed to perceive it.'[4] Galot's chief court of appeal throughout his book is, however, Holy Scripture. On it he bases his stress upon the personal suffering of the Son of God, upon the *kenosis* (understood not as an abandonment of the divine nature, prerogatives, or attributes of the Son but as a renunciation, in his human existence, of the *exercise* of divine attributes), upon the passion as the summit of the incarnation, and upon the deep theological significance of the dereliction on the cross. Here, as in Galot's earlier christological writing, I must admit to finding a point of difficulty, when he speaks of the incarnation as if it resulted from a decision made by the Logos *from within the temporal order*. Thus he writes, with reference to the famous 'kenotic' passage in Philippians 2:

> The voluntary humiliation of the passion in the obedience of the cross is presented as the completion of the movement of the incarnation, the movement of self-annihilation or self-stripping. Now this stripping cannot be attributed to the man in Jesus, since it consisted, for one who possessed the divine condition, in taking a human condition and in particular the condition of a slave. The very act of the incarnation is conceived as a sacrifice, a sacrifice which could have as its subject none but the divine person of the Son.[5]

Apart from the fact, which Galot admits, that many exegetes interpret the 'kenotic' statement as referring not to the act by which the eternal Word becomes incarnate but to the act by which the incarnate Word offers himself for suffering and death, Galot appears in this passage to be assuming that the

Word in his divine nature exists and makes decisions in time. I shall return to this point later on; at the moment I will merely refer the reader to the criticism which I have made elsewhere,[6] only stressing that it does not affect the general movement of Galot's argument.

I find especially enlightening Galot's insight into the significance of the word of desolation 'My God, my God, why hast thou forsaken me?' In his earlier writing he has stressed the implications for the human consciousness of Jesus of the use of the vocative '*Abba*, Father', and he has suggested, though perhaps less emphatically than Karl Rahner and Louis Bouyer, that Jesus, in his earthly life, knew his personal divine status not by having it as the immediate object of his human consciousness but in his consciousness of the Father as the direct object of his filial, and at the same time co-equal, relationship.[7] Here he hints that in the desolation Jesus' consciousness of God as God—*Eloi*—persists but his consciousness of God as Father has been withdrawn, until it returns in the final word 'Father, into thy hands . . .': 'After saying "*Eloi*" in the depth of innermost grief, he says "Father" in the act of trusting self-commitment.'[8] And Galot takes the argument a further step forward.

While stressing that, although the triune God in his totality is causally concerned in the production of the incarnation, it is only the Son who is the personal subject of the human activities and states, Galot points to the significance of the fact that the Son who is their personal subject is the person who is in unbroken filial responsiveness to the Father:

> If the Son suffers as Son, in his relations with the Father, the Trinity is concerned in a mysterious way with this suffering. Far from limiting the suffering to the relations of man with God, the dereliction shows us how, in a certain sense, it is introduced into the heart of God, in the intimacy of the Son with the Father.[9]

And hence, together with his insistence that

> it is the Son, in his capacity as Son, and not only as an incarnate divine person, who has experienced the pains of the passion. The act which consummates this passion, the act of death, is the filial act by which Christ commits his spirit into

the hands of the Father; the filial note is essential in this abandonment,[10]

he also asserts that 'the suffering of Christ poses the problem of the sharing of the two other divine persons in the Passion',[11] and he devotes over fifty pages to an eloquent and moving chapter on the involvement of the Father in the incarnation and the passion; this is followed by an equally long chapter on the suffering of God through the offence caused by sin. Both are based upon an exhaustive study and exposition of Scripture and, although a detailed reproduction of it is unnecessary for our present purpose, it may be thoroughly recommended in its own right. Two conclusions emerge. The first is that the attribution of pain and suffering to God is not to be understood as purely metaphorical, although, like other attributions, it must be interpreted analogically. Thus, Galot writes:

> We must purge the notion of offence of all the imperfections which can characterize human offences. This will allow us at the same time to grasp better the sense in which God suffers from sin; this can only be in an exalted sense, appropriate to the sovereign divine perfection.[12]

The second conclusion is that no concession is to be made to demands for a finite or mutable God; quite the contrary. His willingness to suffer is itself an exercise of his sovereignty:

> God is not subject of necessity to suffering. If he suffers, it is because he has himself decided to be involved in this role and has decided it with all the transcendent freedom which he possesses. . . .
> Of himself, in his divine nature, he is invulnerable. . . . The Bible shows us precisely how, by the covenant, he has made himself vulnerable. . . . It is true that, once involved in this covenant, he can no longer withdraw, because he has forbidden himself to do so. . . . But this suffering which he cannot but undergo belongs to a love which has been willed entirely freely, without any constraint or inner necessity. . . .
> In consequence, to those who hold that suffering is impossible in God it must be replied that such an impossibility, which at first sight would seem to manifest the absolute divine sovereignty, would not preserve it sufficiently. We

cannot refuse to God the sovereign power to expose himself to suffering in free relations of love with men.[13]

Nevertheless, Galot continues, for all its literal reality God's suffering does not diminish him in any way. Simply because his love for man is entirely free, when he loves his perfection is not increased and when he is not loved it does not undergo diminution, and even if a sinner wishes to damage God he succeeds only in damaging himself. God's immutability is absolute, and it is an ontological and not merely a moral immutability.

Up to this point Galot has expounded and defended the reality of the divine compassion and has insisted on its compossibility with divine immutability, but he has not yet exhibited the rationality of his position. This lack he now proceeds to supply, and he takes as his starting-point the fundamental distinction between the divine *being* which is neither lessened nor damaged and the divine *love* which is wounded by the hostile attitude of the sinner. 'In God', he asserts,

> we must recognize an affectivity turned towards men, and it is there that suffering is situated, both that which results from the offence and that which is embedded in the redemptive sacrifice. When the divine persons suffer in their affectivity they do not undergo any wounding in their divine being.[14]

Galot recognizes that to make this distinction between the divine being and the divine love or affectivity will seem to some theologians to contradict the principle of the divine simplicity, for which God's being and his love are really identical. He has however an answer to give. First, he stresses that we are here concerned not with the eternal intratrinitarian love, which certainly falls under the concept of necessity, but with the love of God towards his creatures, which is equally certainly free. 'The sovereign freedom of the love of God towards men is a principle unceasingly made clear by Scripture; the whole doctrine of the gratuitousness of grace and salvation derives from it.'[15] (He might well have added that an essentially similar problem is raised by the very fact of creation; St Thomas Aquinas himself had to try to cope with it.[16] How is the voluntary act by which God wills creatures included in the necessary act by which he wills himself?) Secondly, says Galot—and he says it more than once—'suffering is possible only in the domain of this free and gratuitous love; it cannot annul the fundamental difference which remains between this love and the necessary being of God.' And so 'it cannot cause any diminution or harm to the divine essence.'[17] And, of course, the mystery remains.

It would be outside our present concern to follow out in detail the way in which Galot develops and applies his doctrine to the question of redemption and to the contemporary religious situation. But it is important to stress how obstinately he maintains the principle of divine impassibility.

> People too easily suppose [he writes] that any kind of suffering would destroy the principle of the divine impassibility. But the God who suffers remains the impassible God. There is no contradiction between these two aspects of God, because impassibility is a property of the divine nature, while suffering concerns solely the free love of the divine persons for men.[18]

Indeed, he adds:

> The persistence of the impassibility is necessary in order to elucidate the divine suffering. The mysterious greatness of this suffering comes from the fact that it is the suffering of God; if it was not the suffering of an impassible God it would lose its own value.[19]

Finally, we may note that, on the subject of redemption, there is a total repudiation of those views of the atonement which set a just but angry Father over against a compassionate and suffering Son:

> There is no contradiction between the two roles held by the Father in the work of redemption: the role by which he gives his Son in sacrifice and that by which he receives the redemptive offering of his Son. . . .
>
> Nor is there any contradiction between the two roles held by Christ: the one which consists in revealing and witnessing to the love of the Father for humanity and the other which consists in lifting up to the Father humanity's homage of

reparation. For even in his sacrifice Christ is at once both the gift of God to man and the gift of man to God. . . .

Thus, even in the act of offering his suffering to the Father, Christ expresses and reveals the suffering of the Father himself.[20]

What judgement now must we pass upon this extremely impressive work of Père Galot? First of all, we must note that the problem to which he has explicitly addressed himself—that of the divine impassibility—is only one aspect, though for many it is from the religious point of view the most important and urgent aspect, of the wider, basically philosophical, problem of the divine immutability. The ultimate question is whether, and if so how, a self-sufficient God can be really concerned with the existence and vicissitudes of a changing world and a suffering humanity. It is, as I see it, his great achievement to have made it possible for the Christian pastor or evangelist to speak, with full conviction and without any mental reservations, about the love and compassion of God the Father and at the same time to hold firmly to the metaphysical principles which he may have acquired from his studies in philosophical theology.

The question may, however, arise in some minds whether in developing this line of thought Galot has weakened one of the most effective arguments for the orthodox Chalcedonian Christology, namely that the assumption of a complete human nature by the pre-existent divine person of God the Son has made it possible, *as no other relation between Godhead and manhood could*, for God, without any detriment of his deity, to become, really and not just metaphorically or symbolically, the subject of a human life and to undergo the human experiences of joy and sorrow, suffering and death. When orthodox fathers wrote, with reference to the incarnation, that 'God has suffered' and that 'One of the Trinity has suffered' was it not their deliberate meaning that only the Son has suffered and that he has suffered only as the subject of his human nature? The point must be conceded; neither the Father nor the Spirit was condemned by Pilate nor nailed to the cross, nor did either of them rise from the dead on the third day. Nevertheless, some qualifications need to be made. In limiting the *human* experiences of God to the Person of the Son, and in him to the sphere of his human nature, we are not depriving

God of all other concern with his creation. No one would
maintain, I imagine, that God's love for his world was non-
existent until the Word became flesh and then existed only
within the human life of Jesus. It has, I think, now become
more clearly recognized that, even in the sphere of the incarnation, although only the Son is the personal subject of the
human nature of Jesus, the Father and the Spirit are both involved in their proper and characteristic ways; both Rahner and
Galot maintain as much,[21] and there would not, I think, be
much support today for the view that any one of the three
Persons might equally well have become incarnate but that, one
particular one having done so, the other two have no further
interest in the matter. And indeed, it is precisely from the
starting-point of the personal incarnation of the Son—the
hypostatic union or unity—that Galot moves into the wider
background of the involvement of the Father in the incarnation
and the passion. It might be suggested—though I do not think
that Galot says this in so many words—that it is precisely the
love of the three Persons, each in his proper way, for the
creation, and within the creation specially for man, that
provides the ontological basis which makes it possible for the
Second Person to become the subject of an actual human life.
To revert to Dr Weinandy's terminology, the fact that the
incarnation involves an actual-mixed-relation does not exclude
there being actual-mixed-relations on the ontologically prior
level of creation; it may in fact demand this. There is no doubt
room for a great deal of further discussion in this area; but I do
not think that Père Galot can be justly accused of any disloyalty
to the classical theological tradition. There are, however, two
weaknesses on which I have commented in my earlier consideration of his Christology and whose correction immensely
strengthens his fundamental argument. The first is a tendency
to speak as if the divine Logos, not only in his human but also
in his divine nature, exists in time and makes decisions in time.
Thus he never seems to be quite explicit that what we rightly[22]
describe in our temporal language as *pre*-existence is in fact
timeless existence, just as what we describe as divine *fore*-
knowledge is in fact timeless knowledge. (This, of course, does
not reduce the pre-existence of the Logos to a merely ideal or
conceptual existence in the mind of God;[23] quite the contrary.)
And secondly, without discarding any part of the previous

argument, it cannot, in my opinion, ultimately survive unless it receives as its keystone a more thorough recognition of what we might call the quantitative disparity between God and creation, a disparity which is based on the qualitative contrast between the self-existence of God and the entire dependence of created being upon him. I will make the point in the words of my book *The Openness of Being*:

> Even when we have said that the creation of the world is a timeless act of unconditioned will on the part of God, does not the existence of the world add something to God's own existence and therefore, however timelessly, make God different from what he would be without that timeless act? The answer to this problem lies, I believe, not, as in the former case, in the contrast between God's timelessness and the world's temporality, but in the contrast between God's infinity and the world's finitude. God's presence to the world makes all the difference conceivable to the world—the difference between existence and non-existence—but in the strict sense, the presence of the world to God makes no difference in God; and this, not because the world is any less in God's sight than it is in its own, but because God himself is infinitely more. Finitude and infinity simply do not add together; or, if this is too mathematical a manner of expression, let us say that dependent and self-existent being do not add together; and this, not because there is no link between them but for the precisely opposite reason that it is from its dependence upon self-existent being that dependent being derives its character as dependent. That there is mystery here we gladly affirm, but it is not absurdity, for we can see that in the mystery the answer lies hidden. But let us be quite sure of this: that if we mitigate the mystery in the least degree in the hope of making understanding easier, we shall defeat our own purpose, and absurdity will be the penalty. Admit the tiniest element of time into God's timelessness, admit the tiniest element of finitude into God's infinity, admit the tiniest element of dependence into God's self-existence, and the very existence of the temporal, finite and dependent world becomes altogether inexplicable and unintelligible.[24]

Paradoxical as it will no doubt appear to many, my conclusion is that the reconciliation between the impassibility and the compassion of God depends on each of these two divine attributes being understood in the fullest and most unqualified sense. Over twenty years ago I wrote a small work which must now be almost completely forgotten,[25] in which I maintained and illustrated the thesis that 'on the cardinal points of Christian doctrine orthodoxy consists in holding together two notions which might well seem to be incompatible.' I explained this as follows:

> I do not mean that they are incompatible in fact; the idea that Christianity involves believing contradictions seems to me to be as stultifying and immoral as the view that it involves clutching at one of the horns of any ostensible dilemma. A naïve 'both-and' programme and a naïve 'either-or' programme both provide scope for theological pyrotechnics but little for steady illumination. My point is simply (1) that the two notions may very well *seem* to be incompatible; (2) that if we assume that they are *really* incompatible we shall be tempted to opt for one of them to the exclusion of the other and so to fall into error; but (3) that if we go on to inquire how they must be understood if they are *not* to be incompatible we shall acquire a very much more profound understanding of the question at issue than we had when we began.[26]

And I illustrated this from the history of Christian doctrine by discussing in detail four particular dualities: dependent reality (Creation); derived equality (the Trinity); unconfused union (the Incarnation); and deified creaturehood (Grace). To these I would now add the duality of divine impassibility and compassion, about which I have learnt so much from Thomas Weinandy and Jean Galot.

4 *Quicunque Vult? Anglican Unitarians*

I have remarked elsewhere[1] that a great deal of modern Christology is inspired by a mainly unconfessed and certainly uncriticized mixture of unitarianism and adoptionism. There is nothing surprising in the fact that these two heresies (for that is how Christian tradition in both East and West would describe them) should go together; for, as a matter of history no less than of logic, it was the Church's understanding of the deity of Jesus that led to the explicit formulation of her doctrine of the triune God. In the past, however, it was uncommon for English theologians, if they were Anglicans, to repudiate explicitly either the incarnation or the Trinity; however much their critics might suspect them of unsoundness on these central matters, they themselves usually claimed simply to be giving them a more satisfactory exposition in the light of modern methods of scholarship and of modern scientific knowledge of the universe. With Dr Hensley Henson they would say, if they were put to it, that they could 'repeat and accept the words of the Creed *ex animo*',[2] 'meaning by that that they believed what they took to be its essential meaning.'[3] And having extracted this kind of admission from them, the authorities of the Church were usually not over-anxious to inquire what essential meaning essentially meant. And the theologians in question had themselves for the most part some sense of obligation in their own consciences to the very explicitly incarnational and trinitarian language of the liturgy by which many of them were committed to worship as priests of the Anglican Church.

Things are very different today. The recent symposium *The Myth of God Incarnate*,[4] five of whose seven authors were Anglican priests, was universally seen to repudiate the doctrine of the incarnation as that had always been understood, namely as asserting that Jesus of Nazareth was, and is, God incarnate in human nature. Whether the incarnation could be welcomed as a 'myth' they were not altogether agreed, partly because they were not agreed as to what they meant by the word 'myth'. Some of them apparently ascribed to the idea of the incarnation some symbolical or poetical 'truth' which makes its

entertainment psychologically, spiritually, or morally beneficial
to the religious consciousness of mankind, provided that any
suggestion that it expresses any objective fact is firmly ruled
out. But at least one of them looked on it as positively per-
nicious in any case and blamed it for practically all the crimes
that have been committed throughout Christian history.[5] They
were, however, all agreed that, in the ordinary dictionary sense
of the word 'myth', that is to say a purely fictitious narrative
(OED), the incarnation is a myth and is simply *not true*. Here,
however, I am concerned not primarily with the doctrine of the
incarnation but with the closely associated doctrine of the
Trinity, and in this regard we have an interesting and, as far as I
know, a unique situation. In 1976 the Regius Professors of
Divinity in the two ancient English universities, both being
priests of the Church of England, declared explicitly their
inability to believe in the Trinity. 'I cannot with integrity say',
wrote Dr M. F. Wiles at Oxford, 'that I believe God to be one
in three persons.'[6] And Dr G. W. H. Lampe, from Cambridge,
declared at the end of his Bampton Lectures: 'I believe that the
Trinitarian model is in the end less satisfactory for the articulation of our basic Christian experience than the unifying
concept of God as Spirit.'[7] These are as unambiguous as
statements of the unitarian position as one could hope to find
and, since Dr Lampe devoted his Bampton Lectures to its
advocacy, I propose to consider them at some length.

I am in no position to question Dr Lampe's knowledge of the
New Testament and of the early Fathers; he was after all the
final editor of the Patristic Greek Lexicon. I am, however,
disposed to question the interpretation which he placed upon
the whole movement of life and thought which came to expression in the biblical and patristic corpus. And there are in
fact two quite plain dogmas in terms of which he assessed,
corrected, and in the main rejected the historic belief of
Christendom. The first dogma is that God is one person, not
three, and that the Spirit is therefore not a distinct divine
person but is simply the unipersonal God—the Father—in his
activity towards, and in, the world; hence the title of the
Lectures, *God as Spirit*. The second dogma is that Jesus is not
the eternal Son and Word, the second person of the Trinity,
incarnate in human nature—how could he be, if there is only
one person in God?—but is simply a man in whom God as

Spirit was uniquely and incomparably active. That is to say, Dr Lampe, as he declared himself in his lectures, was both a unitarian and an adoptionist and he was much more lucid and uncompromising in stating his position than many who share these views. In fairness both to him and to his public I shall describe that position as far as possible in his own words.

Dr Lampe opened his discussion by saying that there are two affirmations which in their different ways sum up the attitude of Christians towards the person of Jesus, one from the first century—'Jesus is Lord', the other contemporary—'Jesus is alive today.'[8] And these, he affirmed, raise the christological problem in two of its aspects, how Jesus is related to God and how he is related to us as believers today; with the subsequent question of the light which this twofold relationship of Jesus throws upon God's relation to men both before and apart from him. In spite of Dr Lampe's caveat that 'the question is not whether we should reject the model of Incarnation as the key to Christology and replace it with the model of inspiration' (a concession which hardly seems justified by his subsequent argument), he claimed that 'to answer this basic Christological question the concept of God as Spirit seems to provide a more satisfactory theological model than that of God the Son' and he made the highly provocative remark that 'the Nicene denial that God the Son is other than God the Father, except in a sense which it was ultimately found impossible to determine, prevented a fully personal meaning being given to the assumption of human nature by God the Son' (12f). (I shall later on criticize Dr Lampe's application of the notion of 'model' to Christian doctrines; it is endemic to his work and is, in my opinion, disputable and often misleading.)

'The central conviction of all Christians', said Dr Lampe, 'is that Christ is the focal point of the continuing encounter between God and man which takes place throughout human history' (13). Nothing could be less open to dispute; it is when we inquire what takes place in that encounter that the problems arise. And then we see that, with Dr Lampe as with other theologians, soteriology and Christology are closely connected; what Jesus is believed to be and what he is believed to do are not easily separated even in thought. And quoting from Professor Peter Baelz Dr Lampe asserted: 'Christians see in Christ the ground for trusting and hoping in God, the example of trusting and hoping in God, and the source of inspiration and power to trust and hope in God. This is the essential Christian belief which a Christology using "God as Spirit" as its key concept must fully articulate' (14). He did his best to forestall accusations that his soteriology was merely exemplarist. 'It has been broadly agreed', he wrote, 'that Jesus did not only announce the saving action of God; he himself was the agent by whom it was brought into effect. "Only God can save." "Jesus saves." These are the premises of the Christological syllogism.' Nevertheless he immediately added: 'Yet it is not enough simply to repeat the conclusion, "Therefore Jesus is God." Nor is it anything but highly misleading to infer from that conclusion that the only model for Christology that can satisfy the requirements of soteriology is that of the incarnation of a pre-existent divine being, the Logos who is God the Son' (14).

Am I right in suspecting some evasiveness and ambiguity here? That it 'is not *enough*' simply to repeat that Jesus is God may be true; but is it therefore *false*? The following sentence appears to presuppose that Dr Lampe held it to be true, for one would hardly protest at misleading use being made of a proposition which one held to be false; one would simply reject the proposition. Nevertheless there are ample grounds in the sequel for holding that Dr Lampe did not believe that Jesus is God.

What, however, are the 'requirements of soteriology' to which reference has been made? After outlining some of the imaginative forms in which salvation has traditionally been depicted, Dr Lampe continued:

> If these traditional pictures, or any others which depict salvation as a decisive act of God performed at a definite point in history, represent that which God has done for us in Jesus, then no doubt the best model for Christology is the divine person of the pre-existent Son who comes down into the world of human sin and demonic tyranny. . . . If, however, we reject these myths of redemption, we may give a different answer to the question, 'What has God in Jesus done for man that man himself could not do?'

We do reject these pictures; first, because, not to mention the fact that they receive, on the whole, little support from the New Testament writers, they render it impossible to make sense either of God's revelation to Hosea and Jeremiah or of the evangelists' reports of the teaching of Jesus; secondly, because it is hard to see how the salvation of man, understood in any but a very superficial sense, can be effected in a single act of God in history. (15f)

This is a key passage to Dr Lampe's thought, and it contains several highly questionable assumptions. First, it takes for granted that belief in the pre-existence of Jesus arose purely as the improvisation of a myth or model to give body to previously held views about the nature of salvation. Secondly, it assumes that there is no substantial support for this belief in the New Testament and especially none in the Gospels. The hazardous character of these assumptions was impressively shown by Dr C. F. D. Moule in his recent book *The Origin of Christology*, in which he emphasized the close link that there is in the New Testament between the personal pre-existence of Jesus and his resurrection. (We shall later on notice Dr Lampe's extraordinary attempt to minimize the significance of the resurrection.)

I want to say [wrote Dr Moule] not only that, 'as a result of him [sc. Jesus]' they experienced a new world; but that they experienced Jesus himself as in a dimension transcending the human and the temporal. It is not just that, owing (somehow) to Jesus, they found new life; it is that they discovered in Jesus himself, alive and present, a divine dimension such that he must always and eternally have existed in it.[9]

And, far from it being the case that the pre-existent divine Jesus was invented as the subject of a variety of myths about salvation, it would be far truer to say that the myths (if that is what we are to call them) were constructed as analogies in the attempt to describe the salvation that his followers had found in Jesus.

Dr Lampe's second objection—that it is hard to see how the salvation of man can be effected in a single act of God in history—is a sheer *petitio principii*. Does anybody—in particular anybody who believes that the Old Israel was the *praeparatio evangelica* for Christ—hold that what was done in the death and resurrection of Jesus was the one and only salvific act of God, and not rather that it was the supreme salvific act on which all others focus or from which they radiate, and in which they find their fulfilment and their meaning? It would in any case be wrong to suppose that Dr Lampe was arguing for a multiplicity of acts of God in the religions of mankind in any other than a subjective and indeed a quite arbitrary and fictitious sense.

> It is not [he wrote] . . . the event itself which evokes repentance and therefore has saving efficacy; it is the interpretation which may be put upon it. *It is in fact a particular interpretation placed upon an event which makes it into an 'act of God'*, that is, an event through which a person finds himself confronted by transcendent grace, judgement, claim, demand, calling. There is thus no event, however apparently miraculous, which can in itself compel every observer of it, whatever his presuppositions, to acknowledge it to be an act of God; nor is there any event, however apparently ordinary, which may not in certain circumstances be an act of God for someone. (17)

In spite of the words which I have italicized, I find it difficult, in view of Dr Lampe's book as a whole, to think that he really meant to imply that God is entirely absent from the world's processes except when, by a personal decision, we posit him there; that would imply that we can actually *create God*. But I suspect there is something significant in the fact that, even by a piece of slipshod writing, Dr Lampe could use as synonymous the phrases 'make an event into an act of God' and 'acknowledge an event to be an act of God'. There is at least a suggestion that God's universal presence as creator and sustainer hardly merits description as an act of God unless we have interpreted it as such. And even so the interpretation is not that God has acted or even that the person involved has been confronted by 'God'; only that he 'found himself confronted by transcendent grace, judgement, claim, demand, calling'. Was the omission of mention of God here due to a desire to include the experience of 'anonymous Christians' and indeed of 'anonymous atheists'? It is worth remarking that if one holds that what makes an act an act of God is that God has acted in it one has no difficulty in holding that God may often be active where his activity is unrecognized; if, on the other hand, one holds with Dr Lampe that it is not God's activity in an act but somebody's interpretation of the act that makes it an act of God, one is left with the questions 'whose interpretation?' and 'what interpretation?'; and I suspect that this is what accounts for Dr Lampe's catalogue, from which God is absent and in which it is not even made clear whether the items are necessary constituents or simple alternatives. If it should appear that criticism such as this is mere quibbling and hair-splitting, I must reply that in a matter of such importance as this accuracy both of thought and of expression is highly desirable, and the more so when we are concerned with matters that in any case lie at the limits of human understanding. It is, however, clear that for Dr Lampe the only difference between the world of the Christian and that of the atheist lay in the difference between the interpretations which they severally place upon the world and upon the events composing it. He was in effect expressing the same outlook as that of his fellow anti-incarnationalist and unitarian Dr M. F. Wiles, who has written:

> Particular events by virtue of their intrinsic character or the results to which they give rise give (like the beauty of the lilies) particular expression to some aspect of God's creative purpose for the world as a whole. They are occasions which arouse in us, either at the time or in retrospect, a sense of divine purpose. But that sense does not necessarily entail any special divine activity in those particular events. . . .
>
> Talk of God's activity is, then, to be understood as a way of speaking about those events within the natural order or within human history in which God's purpose finds clear expression or special opportunity.[10]

The only difference seems to be that Dr Wiles appears to hold that God is in fact anonymously operative throughout nature and history, though the discernment of this operation depends on our occasional sensitivity to it (he describes his belief as a form of deism), while Dr Lampe, at least in some of his statements, apparently held that God is present and operative only if we interpret him as being so.

Together with his rejection of salvation as effected in a *single* act of God in history, Dr Lampe, as we have seen, rejected the notion of salvation as depending on a *decisive* act of God in history, without apparently recognizing that the two notions were not identical. But both rejections were coherent with his repudiation of the incarnation. And it seems clear that, like Dr Wiles, he hoped that a form of Christianity which did not affirm particular interventions on the part of the Creator would be congenial to the scientific mentality, which seeks for wider and wider generalizations and is uncomfortable with recalcitrant singularities (compare M. Jacques Monod's embarrassment at the emergence of life and his welcoming of 'chance' as a *dea in machina*!).[11]

It is not really surprising that, with such a starting-point as this, Dr Lampe found it difficult to account for the unique position which he wished to give to Jesus; we might indeed be surprised that, with such a starting-point he should wish to give Jesus a unique position and that he should not be content, with Dr Hick, Dr Wiles, and Dr Nineham in their latest phase,[12] for Jesus to take his place on more or less equal terms with the other great figures of world religion, or even, with Dr Nineham, to entertain the hypothesis that Jesus, as a figure of a past epoch, is not of any special relevance to us today. In any case it is significant that Dr Lampe side-tracked the question who or what Jesus is and substituted for it the question what God has done in him for us. Thus he wrote:

> If, then, we ask again, 'What has God in Jesus done for man that man himself could not do?', our answer can be: 'Created him'; or, rather, 'Brought the process of creation to the point where perfect man appears for the first time.' 'Perfect', in this context, means 'perfect in respect of his relationship to God.' (17)

Dr Lampe added—and here his particular form of unitarianism becomes explicit:

> Creation is a continuing process, and for God's continuous creation of man in ever deeper and richer communion with himself the model of God as Spirit is very apt; for the term 'Spirit' properly refers, not to God's essence but to his activity, that is to say, his creativity. (ibid.)

On Dr Lampe's own principles there appears to be no theological reason why some other man or men should not be—or indeed have been—as perfect as Jesus *and in the same sense*, and if there is no such theological reason it would seem overwhelmingly probable, given the number of human beings who have already lived, that somewhere or other it would have happened. Nevertheless, when it came to the crunch, Dr Lampe was reluctant to draw this conclusion, as we shall see. He explicitly denied that God was uniquely incarnate in Jesus: 'God has always been incarnate in his human creatures, forming their spirits from within and revealing himself in and through them'; yet he held that 'In this continuous incarnation of God as Spirit in the spirits of men the Jesus presented to us by the Gospels holds his unique place.' And again: 'In Jesus the incarnate presence of God evoked a full and constant response of the human spirit.' Nevertheless, 'this was not a different divine presence, but the same God the Spirit who moved and inspired other men, such as the prophets. It was not a different kind of human response, but it was total instead of partial.' (23f) How, then, can Jesus have any effect upon us? Clearly, we must presume, only by setting us an example, and Dr Lampe in fact admitted this:

> If we go on to ask how this affects the rest of mankind, including ourselves, the reply will be that Jesus became both the pattern of sonship and also the inspiration and power which can create in us a response, analogous to his own, to the Spirit of God that was in him and is in us. The interaction of divine Spirit with human spirit presents itself to us, and takes effect within us, in terms of the character, actions, and words of Jesus. (24f)

This is, as no doubt Dr Lampe would have admitted, sheer exemplarism, but he ignored without comment the historic witness of Christendom that, in order to be reconciled to God, man needs something more from Jesus than the example of someone whose life was so perfect that he himself needed no reconciliation at all. But even so, there was a further problem for Dr Lampe of which he seemed quite unconscious.

If we are to be inspired by the example of Jesus' character, actions, and words, we must at least know what that character, actions, and words were; and we can, given Dr Lampe's presuppositions, know this only from the records of them which his contemporaries made and the impression which he made upon them, that is to say, from the New Testament scriptures. And if Dr Lampe and we ourselves were fundamentalists, that would no doubt satisfy us. But as things were, he could only make the rather lame remark that 'Jesus as represented by the evangelists would have answered our question in different words, which nevertheless express the same reality. The Jesus of the Synoptic Gospels would have told us that what God accomplished through himself for men that they could not do was to prepare them for, and bring them to enter or receive, his Kingdom.' (25) But, since Dr Lampe would not have accepted the Jesus of the Synoptic Gospels as reliably representing the real Jesus, or his teaching about the Kingdom as either easy to ascertain ('In the Gospels this term is used with a considerable variety of meanings', 25) or acceptable without considerable demythologizing, it seems difficult, to say the least, to find a convincing basis for Dr Lampe's desupernaturalized Jesus in the New Testament. When he writes that 'the term [sc. "the Kingdom of God"] can be quite properly detached from its associations with first-century apocalyptic and used to answer the questions "What did God do through Jesus to save us?" and "How, or in what sense, does Jesus save us now?"' and that 'it can serve to express concepts which are everywhere present in Christian thought at all times, though they may be put into many different forms of words' (25), one may perhaps wonder whether Dr Lampe might not have found it simpler to dispense with the term altogether rather than to subject it to so radical a process of redefinition, were it not for his desperate need to find support for his remodelled Christology in the only evidence with which he has left himself, namely the text of the Synoptic Gospels.

For—let us be clear about this—it is not only post-biblical developments in Christology that are rejected in Dr Lampe's Bampton Lectures; large parts of the New Testament have to go as well or at least to submit to radical demythologization. Both the pre-existence and the post-existence of Jesus to his earthly life are unnecessary and his survival of bodily death (and presumably ours too) appears to be irrelevant:

> We do not need the model of the descent of a pre-existent divine person into the world. Nor do we need the concept of a 'post-existent' continuing personal presence of Jesus, himself alive today, in order to interpret our own continuing experience of God's saving and creative work. (33)

If the work of God in Christ is continuous with, and part

of, his creation of human spirits through personal communion with them, then the same model or set of concepts is
likely to be appropriate to express our understanding of
God's relationship to the spirit of man at every stage.
. . . We are free to choose whatever model will serve best for
this purpose. (34f)

I shall say something later on about the appropriateness of the
notion of 'model' as a description of Christian doctrine; I will
here remark only that its use here has made it possible for Dr
Lampe to treat it as a matter of convenience whether we say that
Jesus now exists or not. And here we are confronted with an
issue which is not just a matter of theoretical niceties for
professional theologians but which strikes at the heart of the
religion of the ordinary devout Christian, who is convinced not
only that he is indwelt by a divine Spirit who once indwelt Jesus
but that he is in a living union with Jesus himself. When Bishop
Polycarp was called upon to renounce Christ in the stadium at
Smyrna, he did not reply 'I consider that the model of Christ's
continued existence is appropriate to express my understanding
of God's relation to the spirit of man at the present stage', or
even use words to that effect. He said, 'I have been his servant
for eighty-six years and he has never done me any wrong. How
then can I blaspheme my king who saved me?'

It is difficult sometimes to convince devout laypeople that
unorthodox theologians can really hold some of the outrageous
views that are attributed to them, and one is therefore, if one's
own position is orthodox, easily accused of malicious
misrepresentation. In an earlier, and now largely forgotten
controversy , it was often difficult to persuade people that Dr
Paul van Buren actually held that God had never existed and
that neither Jesus nor anyone else had survived bodily death.
And I think that many will find it hard to credit that Dr Lampe,
as a Christian theologian, saw no need of thinking of Jesus
as personally alive today. It is therefore helpful, though
distressing, to be able to quote his own words, and I do not
think one need apologize for paying a scholar the compliment
of assuming that he meant what he said. In the case of Dr
Lampe, there is of course no question about his belief in both
the existence and the activity of *God*, nor about his admiration
for the character of Jesus as it is depicted in the Gospels, as the

picture of what God as Spirit can do with and in a human being. But we have his own word for it that for him it was quite irrelevant whether Jesus exists or not at the present day, for in either case there is no real relationship between him and us.

Dr Lampe was not prepared to abandon all belief in the existence of Jesus of Nazareth as a man who actually lived in first-century Palestine and to look upon him as a purely mythical figure like Osiris or Rumpelstiltzkin, if only because of the effect that belief in Jesus had had upon the lives of Christians down the ages, though he had paradoxically to recognize that the belief in Jesus that had produced this effect was very different from the belief in Jesus that Dr Lampe himself held. 'There is . . .', he wrote, 'surely no need to abandon the historical Jesus as the actual source of the Christian experience of sonship and of the "fruit of the Spirit"' (103), but this means that he was the historical origin of the Christian movement, not that he is the immediate cause of Christian experience today. And even so, with a notable desire to eat his cake and have it, Dr Lampe continued:

> It is true to some extent that the more we come to know about him in the context of the society and culture of first-century Palestine, the more he becomes a stranger to us. Yet it is easy to exaggerate this strangeness. Jesus the Jew, the apocalyptic enthusiast, the wandering exorcist and miracle-worker, and many other aspects of the figure portrayed in the Gospels, is certainly strange to our world. Yet the idea of the Kingdom of God at least lends itself to reinterpretation, as the New Testament itself demonstrates, on lines which make it of the greatest possible significance to every generation. (103f)

The real question is whether, if we take the Kingdom of God as the one element in Jesus' teaching worthy of preservation (but even so needing radical reinterpretation to make it acceptable in our modern cultural setting), the Jesus who remains bears very much likeness to the Jesus of the Gospels and whether this residual teaching is very different from what can be extracted, by similar techniques of selection and reinterpretation from any other of the great religions of the world. In spite of his reluctance to let the actual human figure of the individual Jesus of Nazareth go—a reluctance which did credit to his personal religion and devotion—in the last resort Dr Lampe seemed forced to admit, like many other radical scholars, that his basic Christian commitment was to an event and not to a person, even if a person seemed to be submerged in that event and there was some hope that up-to-date critical methods might extract some information about him from it. In fairness, Dr Lampe must be quoted at length on this point:

> The Christ event, however, is a complex act of God. The historical Jesus stands at the heart of it, and, although many would dispute this, it seems scarcely possible to account for the origin of this Christ-event, which is really a cluster of events, without an actual Jesus of Nazareth who preached and lived the Kingdom of God in a manner recognizably like that which the Gospel traditions describe. Nevertheless, when we claim that Christ is the centre and climax of the entire creative work of God throughout history, and the focal point which gives meaning to the whole, we are not speaking only of that historical figure and his words and deeds, but of a complex disclosure, focused upon Jesus but not confined to him, of God's dealings with men. (104)

Dr Lampe rightly remarked that 'Jesus was interpreted and reinterpreted in different ways even within the period covered by the New Testament' (105), and he had much to say about this interpretative process. He never seriously considered, however, the possibility that this interpretative process in the New Testament and its continuation in the doctrinal activity of the post-New-Testament Church might be a progressive and co-operative articulation of the Church's reflection upon the teaching and actions of her Lord and her experience of his saving power, and might culminate in a deeper and more coherent expression of that reflection and its understanding. For Dr Lampe these 'interpretations and reinterpretations' in the New Testament were conflicting alternatives, at best dispensable as unnecessary and at worst to be rejected as misleading excrescenses; and, as we shall see, he had no hesitation in repudiating the whole historic movement of doctrinal explicitation with its culmination in the classical formulations of the doctrines of the Trinity and the incarnation and in substituting for it his own type of unitarianism and adoptionism.

Dr Lampe might not seem to be saying anything very controversial when he wrote:

> It is also clear that the Jesus of the Gospels is the 'Christ of
> faith' projected back into the pre-Easter period. The
> historical Jesus is seen through the eyes of those who believed
> in him as the risen and ascended Lord, and the tradition of
> his teaching and of his life and work is interpreted and
> reinterpreted in the light of the Easter faith and in relation
> to the evangelistic, apologetic, pastoral, and disciplinary
> tasks, problems and controversies of the Christian com-
> munity. (105f)

Everything depends, however, on the meaning which is to be
given to the words 'projected' and 'interpreted'. Is it meant
that, in the light of the resurrection, Jesus was *correctly seen* to
have been the 'Christ of faith' even before his crucifixion or that
he was *mistakenly supposed* to have been this? And does
'interpreting' mean understanding *correctly* the character of
Jesus and his work or formulating hypotheses about them which
may or may not be correct? Incidentally, what is the difference
between 'interpreting' and 'reinterpreting' (we have found the
two words together before)? Is reinterpreting simply constructing a second interpretation as an alternative to the former
one, or is it interpreting the former interpretation, or is it an
essentially different process from interpretation? These are not
frivolous or trivial questions; they are raised by Dr Lampe's
proposal to abolish the agelong faith of Christendom.

   Dr Lampe is not the first scholar to suggest that the Easter-
experience coloured radically the evangelists' presentation of
the pre-crucifixion life of Jesus. Dr Wolfhart Pannenberg, to
mention one, held this in a form both less and more
revolutionary than Dr Lampe;[13] *less* in that he held the
resurrection to be both historically true and religiously vital,
while Dr Lampe held it to be religiously harmful and
historically false, *more* in that he held it to have made the pre-
crucifixion Jesus historically inaccessible, while Dr Lampe
apparently held that some of his genuine traits could be ex-
cavated from the narrative. (One should, however, remember
that any statements of Dr Pannenberg must be understood in
the light of his highly idiosyncratic view of the nature of
truth.)[14] Nor, of course, was Dr Lampe the first to suggest that
the selection and presentation of the gospel material was in-

fluenced by the situation and needs of the primitive Church. The important question is whether, when the primitive Church was faced with a difficult problem of belief or conduct, it inquired whether there was anything that Jesus was remembered to have said or done that could help it to make the right decision or whether it decided what it wanted to do and then invented a story about Jesus to justify it. Biblical scholars might well ponder these words by Dr Humphrey Palmer:

> Were the first Christians adept at thinking up stories-of-Jesus to suit a situation in their Church? Form-critics do not show this, but take it for granted in all their reasonings. These reasonings do, however, show how adept form-critics are at thinking up early-Church-situations to suit stories of Jesus.[15]

It is true that Dr Lampe thought that, although it was very doubtful whether many, or indeed any, of the words and acts attributed to Jesus in the Gospels were actually uttered and performed by him, he was at least the stimulator of the movement which produced the stories about them. Thus, having said that we cannot tell whether Jesus actually taught the 'Lord's Prayer' or instituted the Eucharist and that 'we do not cherish the parables or pray the "Our Father" or repeat the Words of Institution because they were spoken by Jesus and because we hold certain prior convictions about his authority' (107), he went on to say that 'we value them because we find truth in them and gain inspiration from them, and we acknowledge Jesus to be uniquely significant because he is either their author or else the originator of the impulse which evoked them from the minds of others—from people whose debt to him was so great that they composed them in his name, as his own' (ibid.). However, in the case of the Fourth Gospel we are told simply that it 'is the work of a mind, or minds, other than the mind of Jesus (for the most part, at least), but inspired by the same Spirit of God that was in Jesus. . . . [The Jesus of the Fourth Gospel] may represent the interaction of God's Spirit with the human spirit of John rather than of the historical Jesus' (ibid.). A careful reading of the rest of the chapter from which these quotations are made—significantly entitled 'Jesus and the Christ-event'—confirms the conviction that for Dr Lampe the Spirit of God—more accurately called 'God as Spirit'—produces in believers an experience similar to that which it produced in Jesus but that there is no other contact between them and Jesus himself. Totally rejecting the distinction which the New Testament itself came to make between Jesus and the Spirit, Dr Lampe asserted that 'Christian experience . . . is not an experience of Christ being presented to us by, or through, another divine agency, but a single experience which can be described interchangeably in "Christ" terms or "Spirit" terms' (117). And the supreme New-Testament offender is St Paul, who, it is alleged, has downgraded the Spirit by making him distinct from the Father and therefore inferior to him, and has aggravated his offence by making Jesus personally divine, so that the Spirit has sunk not even into the second place but into the third. And the other New-Testament authors were accomplices in this crime. Here we have it in Dr Lampe's own words:

> Paul speaks of 'participation' or 'fellowship (*koinonia*) 'in the Holy Spirit' as though this were in some way distinct from 'the grace of our Lord Jesus Christ' and 'the love of God'. . . . The effect of Paul's failure to complete the identification of the Spirit with the present Christ is to assign a 'third place' to the Spirit. . . . This reduction of the Spirit to a second, and very ill-defined, place in God's outreach towards the world could have been avoided if the term 'Spirit' had been allowed to express the totality of God in his creativity: in the whole process of his creative work which has its focus in Jesus Christ and continues now in believers. *Paul and John, however, and the other New Testament writers, were unable to do this because they wished to affirm the personal pre-existence of Jesus Christ as Son of God, the continual personal 'post-existence' of Jesus Christ, resurrected and ascended and also experienced by present believers, and the future return of the ascended Christ in glory.* (118f, italics mine)

The sentence which I have italicized is at least perfectly explicit and it shows how little Dr Lampe felt himself to be committed to New-Testament witness as providing the canon of Christian belief. In the two chapters which succeed it he used all the great wealth of his admitted scholarship to show the part which the great concepts of pre-existence and post-existence played in the Church's attempts from its earliest days to give expression to its memories and its experience of its Lord. And his account of this whole movement is, to me at least, both illuminating and convincing; the remarkable thing is that it did not convince *him*. For him the whole mass of Christian thought, witness, and devotion through the ages from its adumbration in the New Testament itself has derived from one colossal initial error which it has taken nineteen centuries to discern; and whatever else is true about the Spirit, if Dr Lampe is correct it has certainly not led the Church into all truth. When, in Colossians, 'the pre-existent Logos has taken on the identity of the historical Jesus of the gospel events' and when 'in no less striking terms the writer to the Hebrews clothes the pre-existent Son through whom God "made the aeons" in the attributes of cosmic Wisdom' (127), the first step has been taken, according to Dr Lampe, towards 'the classical Alexandrian Christology' in which the reality of Jesus' human nature has been lost:

> According to this Christology, the eternal Son assumes a timeless human nature, or makes it timeless by making it his own; it is a human nature which owes nothing essential to geographical circumstances; it corresponds to nothing in the actual concrete world; Jesus Christ has not, after all, really 'come in the flesh'. (144)

Now this may perhaps be true of certain types of Alexandrian Christology but it is certainly not true of the Christology of Chalcedon, which has surely the best claim to be described as 'classical'. For it was the concern of Chalcedon to insist *both* that the subject of Jesus' human nature was the person of the eternal and divine Logos *and* that his human nature was (and is) concrete, complete, and individual. To treat it as virtually monophysite is grossly unhistorical and is also unfair to such modern Chalcedonians as Louis Bouyer and Jean Galot; what is true is that Chalcedon did not claim to solve all the problems of Christology and that it has shown itself to be fertile of creative theological development at the present day. In support of this assertion, I would refer to the chapter on Christology Today in my *Theology and the Gospel of Christ* and to the chapter on Chalcedon and Christology Today in the present volume. We may admit that Dr Lampe's 'Spirit Christology' 'enables us to say that Jesus is authentically human'; the difficulty is to see how, in spite of his efforts, it gives us grounds for supposing that Jesus means any more to us than any other man. 'For', he wrote,

> when we speak of God as Spirit we are not referring to a divine mediator. The early Church's theology demanded a mediator between God and his creation, and the Logos-Son Christology was developed with the praiseworthy intention of affirming that the mediator was himself of one and the same essence as God the Father. *Yet in fact we need no mediator.* It is God himself, disclosed to us and experienced by us as inspiring and indwelling Spirit (or Wisdom or Word), who meets us through Jesus and can make us Christlike. (144, italics mine)

'In fact we need no mediator'—how far Dr Lampe had moved from his earlier evangelicalism when he wrote his Bampton Lectures! But have we not perhaps in this sentence the key to his later position, and may not his occasional puzzling inconsistencies be the vestigial traces of an earlier and more scriptural faith? Even in this last quotation, where the need of a mediator is categorically denied, what can it mean to say that 'God meets us through Jesus' if Jesus is not in some respect a mediator?

If the significance of Jesus is what Dr Lampe held it to be, it is not surprising that he rejected both the incarnation and the 'model' of pre-existence. And, having done this, it was natural that he should go on to reject the resurrection and the 'model' of *post*-existence. 'It does not seem . . .', he wrote, 'that the traditional belief that the physical body of Jesus left the grave, and that he was seen by, and conversed with, some of his followers makes any significant difference to that experience of believers which Paul described as life "in Christ", "Christ in us", the "Spirit in us", the state of being "in the Spirit"' (145). (St Paul, of course, thought that it made a very considerable difference[16] and Dr Lampe had to admit this, though he wrote some very obscure pages in an attempt to minimize it (pp. 146–9).) In any case, he asserted,

> it does not seem that the present-day Christian's experience of the living Christ, which appears to be identical with experience of God as the Spirit that was in Jesus, is dependent

upon the reliability of the traditions about the resurrection appearances or the empty tomb. Belief in Christ as a contemporary presence does not rest upon an assurance that the resurrection of Jesus actually happened as an event in history. (150)

If we find such a statement as this puzzling, we must remember that, as we have already seen, in Dr Lampe's exposition 'experience of the living Christ' does not mean experience which has Jesus as a living person for its object or experience which has Jesus as a presently active living person as its cause, but simply experience which is similar to the experience which we may suppose Jesus to have had and which is caused by an activity of God as Spirit in us similar to the activity which God as Spirit had in him. For, as we had already been told, in the context of Christian experience 'Christ' does not mean the person of Jesus, but the 'contemporary indwelling divine presence' in us: 'the single reality for which these two terms [sc. "Christ" and "Spirit"] stand is the one God in his relation to human persons' (118).[17] Dr Lampe quite honestly admitted that the New-Testament writers thought of 'a post-existent Jesus who has ascended into heaven', but he maintained that 'the reality of Christian experience' would be the same if 'for us the mode and nature of the life of Jesus beyond death is part of the mystery of the state of all men beyond the grave' (158). And by what at this stage of his argument had become a familiar turn of doctrinal gymnastics, he argued that this need cause no qualms of conscience in regard to Christian spirituality and liturgy. By assuming (a somewhat large assumption!) that 'it is, in fact, impossible to distinguish prayer to Christ from prayer to God conceptualized in terms of his self-disclosure in Christ . . ., once more, it seems clear that Christian devotion does not require the concept of a continuing personal presence of a risen and ascended Jesus' (166).

The position here expressed is markedly different from that held by Dr Lampe in 1966, when, in a radio dialogue with Professor D. M. MacKinnon based on an earlier broadcast sermon,[18] he maintained that, although the empty tomb was a myth, the resurrection was an absolutely objective fact: Christ really did return from the dead in glory and appear to his disciples, although in a spiritual and not a bodily form. In the

Bampton Lectures it is the crucifixion, not the resurrection, of
Jesus that is of supreme importance: 'Faith sees the cross as the
place where the union of God and man was consummated and
the God-man supremely glorified' (153). The resurrection is at
most only an optional extra: 'If the historians' verdict should be
that the grave of Jesus was in all probability found to be empty
on Easter Day, and if we are persuaded that Peter, James, Paul,
and the others actually did see Jesus objectively, this will only
confirm our faith that the cross was God's victory; it will not be
the ground of our faith' (ibid.). It is even suggested that faith is
firmer and more authentic without belief in the resurrection: 'If
Easter were needed in order to ensure us that God set the seal of
his approval on Jesus, this would mean that our faith was
altogether less advanced than that of the heathen centurion'
(155); and St Paul's statement that Christ was designated Son of
God in power by his resurrection from the dead was motivated
by 'Pharisaic presuppositions' which 'we do not share' (ibid.).
Much more than 'the literal question concerning the
whereabouts of Jesus' bones' (158) is involved:

> What we need to ask [wrote Dr Lampe] is whether the
> present experience of believers that they are 'in Christ' is
> directly related to, and dependent upon, a resurrection-event
> in the world of time and space, which took place at a par-
> ticular moment in history—whether, in fact, what we un-
> derstand as the active presence of God, the Spirit who was in
> Jesus, must, rather be understood as a personal presence of
> the resurrected Jesus. . . .
>
> This, however, is surely not so. Belief that death does not
> put an end to God's relationship to his human creatures does
> not depend on an assurance that Jesus was raised from the
> dead. . . .
>
> Belief in future life did not depend for the first Christians,
> and need not for ourselves, upon an Easter event. (159f)

In the pages from which these passages come three quite
distinct matters are confused and identified, namely (1) survival of bodily death, (2) the relationship of all human beings
to God, and (3) the specifically Christian situation of being 'in
Christ'. However, to all of these the resurrection and ascension
of Jesus are declared to be irrelevant, and belief in them to be
pointless and indeed undesirable; and there is no suggestion

that they could be important in any other respect. In particular, their cosmic significance as establishing the supremacy of Christ, and of man in Christ, over the whole created realm of matter and spirit—the theme of the opening chapters of Colossians, Ephesians, and Hebrews—is totally ignored, as indeed it must be, for there is nothing that Dr Lampe's unitarianism can say about it.

I shall not discuss here the consequences which Dr Lampe drew from his premises for the theology of the Church and the sacraments and for Christian spirituality and morality; they naturally follow from his basic doctrines and I have here been primarily concerned to examine his theological foundations rather than his superstructure. I am, however, glad to point to some of the important truths which survive his drastic remodelling of the Christian faith. First of all, the most traditional Chalcedonian will wish to endorse his stress upon the reality of the human nature of Jesus. Frequently as this is forgotten by its opponents, Chalcedonian Christology is just as insistent upon the humanity of Jesus as upon his deity; this carries the consequence, which is strangely inacceptable to many inventors of 'new Christologies' that, radically diverse as deity and humanity are metaphysically, they are not incompatible or antagonistic, since the *same* person, Jesus, *is both God and man*. Secondly, while Dr Lampe was in error in denying the distinct personality of the Holy Spirit, he was right in affirming that Jesus is a totally Spirit-filled man. Thirdly, an orthodox understanding of the Spirit will find even more room than Dr Lampe for the in-dwelling of the Spirit in Christ's members and their energizing by him. The doctrine of the Spirit, like the doctrine of the Trinity, has only too often been neglected and accorded mere lip-service, but the remedy for this is not to be found in the unitarianism of Dr Lampe or Dr Wiles. It is to be found in a full recovery and implementation of the traditional trinitarianism of Christendom.

THE SURVIVAL OF THE TRIUNE GOD

For the Trinity is not primarily a doctrine, any more than the incarnation is primarily a doctrine. There is a doctrine *about* the Trinity, as there are doctrines about many other facts of existence, but, if Christianity is true, the Trinity is not a doctrine; the Trinity is God. And the fact that God *is* Trinity—that in a profound and mysterious way there are three divine Persons eternally united in one life of complete perfection and beatitude—is not a piece of gratuitous mystification, thrust by dictatorial clergymen down the throats of an unwilling but helpless laity, and therefore to be accepted, if at all, with reluctance and discontent. It is the secret of God's most intimate life and being, into which, in his infinite love and generosity, he has admitted us; and it is therefore to be accepted with amazed and exultant gratitude. The way in which the Church, as it reflected on the life, teaching, passion, and resurrection of Jesus of Nazareth and its experience of his liberating and transforming activity, was led to formulate its belief in the best words that it could find is a fascinating subject for Church historians, as also is the ever deepening understanding by the Church through the ages of that belief when formulated. Dr Lampe, in the fifth chapter of his Bampton Lectures, gave a wonderfully comprehensive, erudite and, to my mind, fully convincing account of this process, with its inchoate simplicity, its tentative explorations, its occasional oscillations and divagations, its permanent achievements, and its continual fruitfulness in the life of the Church down the centuries; I part company with him only in his judgement that this whole movement has been radically misdirected and mistaken and in his substitution for the traditional belief in the Trinity and the incarnation of a combination of unitarianism and dynamic monarchianism. Dr Lampe made repeated attempts to retain some kind of uniqueness for Jesus in his system, but it is indeed hard to see what justification he provided for this, and I find myself echoing Mr A. E. Harvey's doubt how long it will be before others, following his line, will question his 'emphasis on the centrality and decisiveness of the action of God in Jesus' (228).[1]

The God whom the Christian Church proclaims is the fundamentally triune God, Father, Son, and Spirit, not a unitarian God to whom the trinitarian character is attached as a kind of secondary, or even optional and purely symbolical, appendage. Admittedly, Western Christian textbooks have frequently divided their expositions under the successive headings *De Deo uno*, dealing with natural theology, and *De Deo trino*, dealing with revealed. But even if this has its advantages from the point of view of apologetics and the wider ecumenism, our understanding of the One God and his relation to the created order is transformed almost beyond recognition when we understand that this One God is the Holy and Undivided Trinity. We may be grateful to Eastern Orthodox writers such as Vladimir Lossky and Dr John Meyendorff for their insistence that a Christian doctrine of God must start and not just end with the Trinity,[2] though we may think that Eastern controversialists have gone too far when they have accused the West, from St Augustine onwards, of depersonalizing God by beginning in its thought with the one divine essence and only remembering in an afterthought that in this one essence there are three Persons.[3] It is significant that the great ecumenical creed of Christendom cannot profess its belief in the One God without immediately identifying him with the Person of the Almighty Father, and going on from this to speak of the Son and the Spirit, who, while distinct as Persons, are consubstantial with him and derive their being from him. It is also interesting to note that Fr Karl Rahner, in a highly characteristic exposition of trinitarian doctrine starting from the notion of 'the free gratuitous self-communication of God to the spiritual creature in Jesus Christ and in the "Spirit"', writes: 'We say: "of God", and we do not presuppose thereby a "Latin" theology of the Trinity (as contrasted with the Greek one), but the biblical theology of the Trinity (hence, in a sense, the Greek one.)'[4] He continues:

> Here God is the 'Father', that is, the simple unoriginate God, who is always known as presupposed, who communicates *himself* precisely when and because his self-communication does not simply coincide with him in lifeless identity. In this self-communication he stays the one who is free, incomprehensible—in a word, unoriginate.
>
> God's unoriginatedness, as manifested in his self-communication, possesses a positive character: the fact that the divine unoriginate communicates himself in no way threatens or impairs his absolute integrity.

Nobody could describe Fr Rahner's mental background as anything but Western; it is therefore ecumenically significant that his writing about the Trinity and the incarnation has received warm approbation from Dr John Meyendorff, who is one of the most creative Orthodox theologians of the present day.[5]

If, then, the great tradition of Christendom is true, the personal God, of unimaginable splendour, bliss, and love, upon whom the world and human beings depend for their existence from moment to moment, is not one solitary monad, but three Persons, united in one life of perfect mutual giving and receiving, a giving and receiving that is so complete that there is nothing to distinguish one from another except the ways in which each gives and receives; a life of sharing so perfect and intense that the most intimate of human unions bears only a remote and analogical comparison to it. And if we wish to acquire some faint understanding of the wonder and glory of the Christian God—who, we must remind ourselves, is the only God there is—we may well find the poets more helpful than the theologians. I have specially in mind Dante, in the final canto of the Divine Comedy, striving to put into words his vision of the triune Godhead, as it smote him in all its dazzling splendour, gathering into its one embrace all conceivable perfections and in its threefold mystery eternally flooding itself with love and satisfying in its mysterious unity every human desire:

> That light doth so transform a man's whole bent
>   That never to another sight or thought
> Would he surrender, with his own consent:
>
> For everything the will has ever sought
>   Is gathered there, and there is every quest
> Made perfect, which apart from it falls short . . .[6]

'Blessed are the pure in heart, for they shall see God'[7] is the promise of Christ in the Beatitudes, and that the end of man is the vision of God has been a commonplace of Christian spirituality down the ages. Nevertheless, God has not revealed himself to us as Holy Trinity simply in order to satisfy our intellectual curiosity or even in order that we shall simply gaze upon his transcendent glory and beauty in spellbound delight, but in order that we shall be taken up into the very life of God himself. As the Fathers repeatedly insist, the Son of God became man that we men might become sons of God, he took our nature that we might be taken into his, he has become what we are that we may become what he is, he was humanized that we might be divinized; and this nature into which we are taken in him is the nature of the triune God. This is the heart of the High-priestly Prayer in the seventeenth chapter of St John's Gospel: 'Father, . . . the glory which thou hast given me I have given to them, that they may be one even as we are one, I in them and thou in me, that they may become perfectly one. . . . Father, I desire that they also, whom thou hast given me, may be with me where I am, to behold my glory which thou hast given me in thy love for me before the foundation of the world.' The Eastern Church has perhaps been most explicit about this, though it has not been absent, as has sometimes been alleged, from the spirituality of the West.[8] The goal of Orthodox spirituality', wrote Vladimir Lossky,

> the blessedness of the Kingdom of Heaven, is not the vision of the essence, but, above all, a participation in the divine life of the Holy Trinity; the deified state of the co-heirs of the divine nature, gods created after the uncreated God, possessing by grace all that the holy Trinity possesses by nature.

And again:

> The Trinity is, for the Orthodox Church, the unshakeable foundation of all religious thought, of all piety, of all spiritual life, of all experience. It is the Trinity that we seek in seeking after God, when we search for the fullness of being, for the end and meaning of existence.[9]

It must not be supposed, however, that trinitarian belief has its implications only in the realm of personal devotion or liturgical practice. It was the inspiration of the great Christian social movement in nineteenth-century England. 'My desire', wrote Frederick Denison Maurice, 'is to ground all theology upon the Name of God the Father, the Son, and the Holy Ghost. . . . This is the method which I have learned from the Bible. There everything proceeds from God; he is revealing himself, he is acting, speaking, ruling.'[10] And that much neglected prophet Thomas Hancock, preaching in 1873, when the Athanasian Creed was under violent attack:

> I believe that our mightiest apologies for the Faith are made when we are not thinking of *it*, but of that God and that humanity, whose union and mediation in the person of Jesus

Christ this creed so wonderfully sets forth. I do not know how to regard the Athanasian Hymn as a 'besieged castle to be defended'; but it seems to me to be a weapon of attack, which may become mighty through God to the pulling down of the strongholds behind which many lies and injustices of our own generation, the evil traditions and corruptions of prior generations lie entrenched.[11]

And again:

There is no certainty that God is the Father unless it be true that he has, and ever has had, a co-eternal Son. We might by a figure of speech call him *a* Father, but *the* eternal and absolute Father he cannot be, unless there is One who is not merely *a* son but the eternal absolute Son.[12]

I would suggest that the chief reason why the Trinity has often appeared as the most abstract of theoretical speculations, suited only for the cobweb-spinning of the remoter type of theologian, is not that it has been taken too seriously but that it has not been taken seriously enough. It has been looked upon simply as a suitable topic for historical research by scholars, while the parish clergy have tended to look on it as far too difficult for them and to take refuge on Trinity Sunday in sermons on what they take to be the easier subject of worship. Rarely is it understood to be the heart and source of the religion by which Christians live. But so it is, and unless they recognize this their religion will be impoverished and stunted. Fr Karl Rahner may not have found the happiest phrase in which to express this when he asserts that 'the economic Trinity is the immanent Trinity',[13] but the point which he is making is vital. It is that the God whom we experience—that is to say, God who communicates himself to us and reveals himself to us—is the God who *really is*, when all allowances have been made for our finite and imperfect mode of understanding. This is the mystery which the Epistle declares, not made known in former generations, the trinitarian mystery revealed by the Father in Christ through the Spirit, not to annihilate or reject the order of creation, but to bring all things into unity in Christ, both things in heaven and things on earth.[14] In the life of this triune God we already share in grace, and we hope, through the divine mercy, to enjoy it fully in glory in the beatific vision in heaven, in the communion of saints, the resurrection of the body, and the life everlasting.

I must now fulfil my promise to discuss Dr Lampe's use of the concept of 'model' to characterize Christian doctrines and in particular the doctrines of the Trinity and the incarnation. It occurs repeatedly throughout his Bampton Lectures and it is, as I hope to show, question-begging and misleading.

The introduction of the term 'model' in theology was, I think, largely due to the late Ian T. Ramsey, originally in the phrase 'models and qualifiers' in connection with the problem of speaking about God,[15] and I doubt whether it added much to the classical theories of analogical predication.[16] But later, both in Ramsey and in other writers, it became associated with the view that theological and religious doctrines are comparable with scientific hypotheses, as rationalizations and systematizations of experience. Now when the term was first used in physical science in the later nineteenth century, it was chiefly in connection with the luminiferous ether and it was understood in a highly realistic and concrete way; for men like Maxwell and Kelvin the ether was conceived as having the same essential properties as gross matter, though the structure which had to be assigned to it became more and more complicated.[17] When, however, such material images were found to be in any case inadequate, first in connection with electromagnetic phenomena and. later with relativistic and quantum phenomena, the notion of 'model' was more and more widely extended until it came to denote not a material and mechanical but a dynamical or even a purely mathematical and abstract structure and when it is now used it has an almost purely heuristic and pragmatic function in correlating and predicting phenomena and is not necessarily thought of as describing concrete reality. A modern physicist would not, I think, use it to describe entities of whose existence he felt fairly confident, such as molecules and atoms; he might be readier to use it of the 'fundamental particles' with their elusive behaviour in the realm of quantum theory and still readier to use it of the still more elusive and hypothetical quarks. At the other extreme of physical magnitude we have the use of the term 'model' for the various schemata with which cosmologists have tried to systematize and predict the large-scale behaviour of the physical universe; thus Dr G. J. Whitrow devoted two chapters to

'World-Models' in his book *The Structure and Evolution of the Universe.*[18] Among scientists themselves the concept of 'model' has a limited and variable application, and I would suggest that it should be used in theology only with great caution and should then be carefully defined. (In any case it is questionable whether the hypothetico-deductive view of scientific theories is more than remotely applicable to religious doctrines, even if, which is far from true, it was universally accepted in its own realm; Dr T. F. Torrance, who has done as much as anyone to defend the claim of theology to be considered as a scientific discipline,[19] has carefully avoided this pitfall.) The notion of 'model' may be useful in certain theological fields, where some reality of faith is analogically comparable, in various limited ways, to a number of diverse finite beings or processes; thus the saving work of Christ is something like winning a battle, something like curing a disease, something like releasing a prisoner, something like repatriating an exile, but not exactly like any one of these. And by using all these models or analogues, defining the limitations of each and bringing them together, as far as possible, into a coherent pattern, we may succeed in acquiring a less inadequate understanding of the Saviour's work than we should have if we used only one of them or refrained from using any of them at all. And the first thing which we need to determine when we are presented with a number of models for some mystery of the faith is whether they are alleged to be mutually exclusive, so that at most one of them is to be adopted, or mutually compatible, so that several or all of them are. An orthodox believer, who maintains that Jesus is both God and man, will have no difficulty in holding both that Jesus is an incarnate pre-existent divine person and also that Jesus is the man in whom the Spirit of God has been supremely manifested and active; though he may not be over-anxious to apply the term 'model' to these two concepts. For Dr Lampe, however, the two were incompatible on *a-priori* grounds; the second was to be accepted and the first was, in consequence, to be rejected. I think that, in any case, the notion of models is not really helpful when we are concerned with the clear truth or falsehood of an assertion, even if its truth does not preclude further wondering and questioning but opens up regions of inexhaustible mystery. To the questions 'Are there three persons in God?' and 'Is Jesus both God and man?'

I do not think it is helpful to reply by talking about the Trinity and the incarnate Son as 'models', though it will help a great deal if we do our best to clarify the meanings of the questions. For, if Christianity is true, the essence of our religion is a personal relation between us and God, and between us and Jesus; and I do not find it easy to have a personal relation with a model. That Dr Lampe had a faint sense of this is perhaps indicated by the fact that, by verbal imprecision of a type not uncommon among theological radicals, he could describe the incarnational christological 'model' on one page (14) as the *act* of becoming incarnate and on the next page (15) as the *person* who becomes incarnate. No doubt, having convinced himself that the traditional Christology 'prevented a fully personal meaning being given to the assumption of human nature by God the Son' (13), it did not seem to him to be unjust to conclude that the object of its devotion was a model; and if, occasionally though more rarely, he used the term 'model' in relation to his own Christology (as when he wrote: 'The model of "Spirit" seems especially suitable for Christology and for interpreting man's whole experience of encounter with God' (12)), we must remember that, as we have already seen, it did not matter to him in the last resort whether Jesus is a person living today, with whom we are in vital relationship, or not. There would seem to be a connection, psychological if not precisely logical, between his basic unitarianism, with its exemplarist soteriology, and his reinterpretation of doctrines as models. However, I hope that the preceding discussion will have shown that, for the understanding of the nature and function of Christian doctrines, 'model' is a very unsatisfactory model indeed. And here I would revert to a point which I made earlier, that the Trinity is not either a doctrine or a theory but a reality, and a reality of which we have experience. In Fr Rahner's words:

When entering upon the doctrine of the Trinity, we need not hesitate to appeal to our own experience of Jesus and his Spirit in us as given in the history of salvation and faith. For here the immanent Trinity itself *is* already present. The Trinity is not merely a reality to be expressed in purely doctrinal terms: it takes place in us, and does not first reach us in the form of statements communicated by revelation.

On the contrary, these statements have been made to us because the reality of which they speak has been accorded to *us*. They are not made to be the touchstone of faith in something to which we have no real relationship, but because our grace and our glory cannot be disclosed to us except in the statement of this mystery. Both mysteries, that of our grace and that of God in himself are the same fathomless mystery. The treatise on the Trinity should never lose sight of this. [20]

And here, I think, we have the clue to the falsity of the assertion which sophisticated theologians are so prone to make, that 'simple believers', who have not been trained in the complexities of scholastic dialectic, are bound to be either modalists or tritheists, and probably the latter. [21] I believe that this is very rarely true, and that when it does occur it is more likely to be with sophisticated theologians than with simple believers. The simple believer knows that the Father is God, the Son is God, and the Holy Spirit is God, and he gives divine honour and worship to each. Also, he has no difficulty in affirming that there is one God and not three, though his capacity of rationalizing this mystery may go no farther than is involved in repeating the trinitarian clauses of the Athanasian Creed, if indeed it goes as far. And the reason for this is not difficult to understand; it is that the simple believer is in fact in living relationship with the triune God and therefore knows him, however obscurely, *as he is*. He may indeed defer to the authority and tradition of the Church for the language in which the trinitarian faith is expressed, but when he accepts it he is conscious that the God it is describing is the God with whom he is himself in living union and whom he knows not just by report but by experience. On the plane of sophisticated theology we have two safeguards against tritheism which we do well to retain. The first is the notion of *perchōrēsis*, the complete mutual interpenetration and sharing of divine life and being by the three Persons, each in his own proper manner; made use of, in the East, by St John of Damascus, translated into Latin as *circumincessio* by Burgundio of Pisa and later given the variant form *circuminsessio*. [22] The second is the notion of the Persons as 'subsistent relations'; elaborated in the West by St Augustine, it has the added advantage that it meets the need, emphasized by Fr Rahner, of pointing to the different characteristics of the Persons and eliminating any impression that the Persons are merely three numerically distinct instantiations of a univocal universal concept of 'personality' or 'personhood'. (Père Galot's variant, 'relational being' (*être relationnel*), makes plain in addition that the Persons have a subsistent and not a merely adjectival status.[23])

But now, in conclusion, to return to Dr Lampe and Dr Wiles. They are entirely right in stressing the humanity of Christ; they are only wrong in denying his divinity. They are entirely right in stressing the unity of God and the deity of the Father; they are only wrong in denying the deity of the Son and of the Spirit. And since, both historically and systematically, there is an extremely close connection between trinitarianism and orthodox Christology, it is not surprising that their extremely reduced Christology and their extremely reduced theism fit quite neatly together. Accordingly, in comparison with the richness and fecundity of traditional Christianity both their Christology and their theism appear sterile and bleak. For all that our leading Anglican unitarians have to offer us in its place is one third of the Church's God and one half of the Church's Christ.

5 *Sexuality and God*

INTRODUCTION

That the one Lord Jesus Christ is literally, completely, and perfectly human is a no less essential truth of the Catholic Faith than that he is literally, completely, and perfectly divine. In the words of the *Quicunque vult*,[1] he is 'equally (*pariter*) both God and man'; he is 'man from his mother's substance, born in time' as truly as he is 'God from the Father's substance, begotten before time'. He is 'perfect man, composed of a rational soul and human flesh', so that, while he is 'equal to the Father in respect of the divinity', he is 'less than the Father in respect of the humanity'. The fact that he is one Christ and not two has indeed been secured by the taking up of humanity into God and not by the conversion of divinity into flesh—how else could it be, when it is God becoming man, and not a man becoming God?—but this has not involved any 'confusion' or blurring of the two natures or 'substances' of divinity and humanity but simply the oneness of the Person whose natures they are. Divinity and humanity, Godhead and manhood, are distinct and unconfused; nevertheless there is but 'one Christ' and he is both God and man.[2] And this humanity, this human nature, this manhood is no fiction or phantom, no logical or psychological abstraction; it is as concrete and fleshly as the manhood which each one of us bears.

I argued in an earlier chapter that, paradoxical as it might appear at first sight, there is no contradiction between the universality of Jesus as the saviour of all mankind and his particularity as one individual first-century Jew, born of Mary at Bethlehem and crucified on Golgotha under Pontius Pilate.[3] I suggested also that the special kind of unity which the human race possesses overflows the limits of the familiar philosophical conceptualizations and contrasts in terms of universals and individuals or particulars and is adequately expressed only in strictly theological terms. I would carry this suggestion into more detail by asserting that the fact that it has been possible for the universal creator to become an individual human being ('fleshed and inhominized' says the Nicene Creed) can presumably tell us a great deal about both the Person who has assumed manhood and the manhood which he has assumed.

I would agree with Fr Karl Rahner and Fr Louis Bouyer[4] that it is a weakness in St Thomas Aquinas to have admitted that *any* one of the three divine Persons *might* have become incarnate, that *more than one* of the divine Persons *might* have become incarnate in the same individual human nature, and that a divine Person *might* have become incarnate in more than one individual human nature,[5] though I think it is fair to recognize that St Thomas appears to be considering only what is possible to the absolute omnipotence of God, which is limited only by what is logically contradictory or is contrary to God's own character. He maintains vigorously that it was much more 'suitable' (*convenientissimum*) that the Son rather than one of the other divine Persons should be incarnate and that human nature was more 'assumable' (*magis assumptibilis*) than any other.[6] And this special 'assumability' of human nature is seen by St Thomas as directly linked with man's creation in the 'image' of God, which is understood as meaning that, as a rational creature, he is 'capable of God', that is, of 'attaining him by the distinct operation of knowledge and love'.[7] In any case, if God the Son *has* assumed manhood, then both God the Son *is* incarnable and manhood *is* assumable. I wish now to devote some space to this manhood which God has assumed.

One of the most obvious facts about human beings is that, even when we have left out of account the fact that some are fully grown while others are infantile, adolescent, or senile, and the fact that some are healthy human specimens while others are physically or mentally defective, they fall into familial, racial, cultural, national, and many other groupings which, although their boundaries may sometimes be difficult to define and may be to a greater or lesser degree flexible and fluid, are nevertheless for various reasons often mutually exclusive. You cannot be a human being without having one pair of parents and not another, without belonging to one racial type and not another, without having one set of aptitudes and not another. And even where two variants of a characteristic are not in principle absolutely mutually exclusive, as, for example, a man may have dual nationality or may change from one nationality to another, or, to take another example, he might conceivably have all the qualities needed for both a prison officer and a classical archaeologist, the sheer finitude of human life in both space and time sets *some* limits to the number of possible

varieties of human behaviour and achievement of which any
man is capable, even among those for which he has some
physical and mental aptitude, to say nothing of those for which,
however well equipped for them some of his fellows may be, he
is himself totally incompetent. No man can enjoy *every*
nationality either simultaneously or successively; not even the
most versatile among us, not even Dryden's Zimri—

> A man so various, that he seem'd to be
> Not one, but all Mankind's Epitome. . . .
> But, in the course of one revolving Moon,
> Was Chymist, Fidler, States-man, and Buffoon . . .

could become, even in the course of one human life, *every* type
of scientist, musician, man of affairs, and the rest. The point
may seem too obvious to need labouring, but it is of theological
importance, primarily in Christology but also for our understanding of a Christian anthropology. For the fact that Jesus
could be the universal saviour of mankind and at the same time
a very special individual Palestinian Jew of what we now desig-
nate from him as the 'first' century, shows that the relation
between the individual and universal aspects of human nature
itself is much more elaborate and mysterious than a superficial
consideration might lead us to suppose.

Differentiation is thus inherent in the unity of mankind, not
inconsistent with it. But this does not mean that the various
human differentiations—familial, racial, cultural, national,
and the rest—do not need unceasing vigilance if they are to be
kept in their right relations with one another or that any one of
them may not be destructive of the unity if it becomes
hypertrophied, distorted, or parasitic. The human species does
not consist of lifeless and passive objects, which can be neatly
and exhaustively classified, according to various *rationes
dividendi*, by their nationalities, racial origins, individual
aptitudes, intelligence-quotients, leisure-interests, psychological types, health prognoses, and so on, and then handed
over to computer-processing for storage with a view to
future utilization if desired; human beings are, beyond all this,
persons with immortal souls and eternal destinies, capable of
horrible crimes and of deeds of colossal and dazzling charity,
fallen through their own sinfulness but redeemed by God in
Christ, and always leading lives that are directed by the

mysterious mutual interpenetration of human free will and divine grace.

SEXUALITY IN MAN

I must now repair one glaring but deliberate omission. There is one human differentiation that is at once so wide in its range and so unique in its character and importance that it needs even in a brief account to receive a separate discussion; I mean the differentiation of sexuality, the distinction between male and female. Not only is this invariable throughout the human species, it permeates all the higher levels of the animal kingdom and a great deal of the vegetable as well. In non-human species it takes a quite amazing variety of forms, some of which are from our point of view extremely bizarre; it is closely instrumental to the maintenance and perpetuation of the species, and in man it is the foundation of the most intense forms of self-giving devotion, both parental and marital, as well as providing the material for some of the grossest forms of vice. Its emotional associations are so varied and intense that it is difficult to find a word to denote it without evoking some at least of these associations. I shall here use the word 'sexuality' in a purely heuristic sense, simply to denote the differentiation of human beings into male and female, and 'sex' and 'sexual' correspondingly; 'sex' will not be a synonym for 'copulation', or 'sexual' for 'erotic'.

The first point which I wish to make about sexuality is that it is far more fundamental, even from an empirical aspect, than any of the other differentiations which I have mentioned. Whether you are Caucasoid, Negroid, or Mongaloid, whether you are German, Costa-Rican, or North-Korean, whether you are a Nobel-prize winner or a failure in all your O-levels, whether your natural aptitude is for all-in wrestling, hospital nursing, or writing Persian erotic verse, you are, basically and genetically, either a female or a male; your sex-chromosomes are either all X or include a Y. (Why I state the matter in this way, rather than in the usual form that the female is XX and male XY, will appear in a moment.) I am, of course, aware that the development and expression of sexual features, both physical and mental, are dependent upon hormonal and other influences which can be modified both deliberately and accidentally, but this does not affect the basic sexual duality rooted in the chromosomes. Some advocates of the admission of women to the priesthood have asserted that sexuality is a purely superficial and secondary adornment imposed on a fundamentally non-sexual human nature. Others have asserted that sexuality is indeed intrinsic to human nature but that, so far from existing in two distinct types, it is a continuous variable (in the mathematical sense) which can take a continuous spectrum of values varying from 100 per cent male at one extreme to 100 per cent female at the other, with the great majority of persons being of intermediate types, x per cent male and y per cent female, where x and y can have any positive values subject only to the condition that $x + y = 100$. Neither of these views has any foundation in modern genetics, which has made it plain that sexuality in mankind is fundamental to its very existence as such, and that it occurs in two quite distinct types, types moreover which are not merely distinct and contrasted but are asymmetrical, in that they are differentiated not by the presence of a different factor in each, as if for example females were just X and males were just Y, but by the presence or absence of one particular factor—Y in males, no Y in females—with a common presence of X in both.

So much imprecise—and, I believe, in the last resort mainly irrelevant—appeal has been made to genetics in current theological controversy that readers to whom modern biological science is unfamiliar may be glad to be informed of the important facts.[1] In each of the cells of the body of a normal human being there are 46 chromosomes, which carry, in a coded form, the inheritable characteristics (or the factors that determine most of these) of the human being concerned. There is an exception in the cells involved in sexual copulation, in which the number is 'reduced' to 23, so that the fertilized cell resulting from the impregnation of the female ovum by the male spermatozoon has the normal number of 46, contributed in equal numbers by the two parents. 44 of the 46 chromosomes in the normal human cell fall into 22 neatly matching pairs; so do the remaining two in females, but not in males. The twenty-third pair—known as the 'sex-chromosomes'—are denoted by the letters X and Y; and the female is therefore symbolized as XX and the male as XY. When 'reduction' (or meiosis) takes place, therefore, every reduced cell from the female will contain an X chromosome as its single No. 23; but half the reduced cells from the male will contain an X and the other half will contain a Y. That is to say, females produce only one kind of ovum, an 'X', while males produce two kinds of sperms, an 'X' and a 'Y'. If now an ovum is fertilized by an X-sperm the offspring to which it gives rise will have the constitution XX and will be female; whereas if it is fertilized by a Y-sperm the offspring will have the constitution XY and will be a male. 'It is for this reason', writes Dr Anthony Smith, 'that the male is the arbiter of an offspring's sex.'[2]

This conclusion is confirmed by certain pathological conditions which have been traced to abnormal numbers of sex-chromosomes. One, where the X is present and the Y entirely absent and which is therefore symbolized as XO, is, as one would expect, an immature female. Most possess, in addition to the normal X and Y, extra X's and/or Y's; thus there are XXX, XXXX, XXXY, XXYY, XYY and even XXXXY. What is striking is that, whenever there are one or more Y's the individual is recognizably male, however many X's there may be as well, while (with possible exceptions mentioned in the note) only in the total absence of Y's is the individual recognizably female, though in both cases some of the characteristics of the other sex may be manifested. In other words, the Y-chromosome, although it seems to play little part in normal genetic inheritance,[3] is extremely influential in the determination of sex.[4]

Some readers will perhaps object that the last two paragraphs, concerned as they are with the purely physical aspect of human nature, are out of place in a theological discussion. I would reassure them by pointing out that Christian theology has consistently maintained that a human being is not a pure spirit, temporarily enclosed in a physical structure with which he has no real affinity, but is a psychophysical unity of an extremely complicated and mysterious type, and that on the physical side of his twofold nature he is organically integrated with the world of matter and in particular with that part of it which is the concern of biological science, including molecular biology and genetics. The theologian will always be wise to refrain from attributing to the dominant theories of geneticists an absoluteness and a permanence which no scientific theories can ever legitimately claim, and the history of science is littered with the remains of theories which in their times appeared to be unshakable and eternal. Nevertheless, while conscious that *all* scientific assertions are subject to revision in the light of further investigations and that this is especially relevant where a large element of interpretation has been involved, we may, I think, make the following remarks fairly confidently:

(1) There are two kinds of normal human beings, male and female, which are clearly contrasted with each other, and not a continuous range from 100 per cent male to 100 per cent female with mixed types of various proportions in between. Genetically, these two kinds are symbolized as XY and XX respectively.

(2) In order to be a normal human being, it is necessary to be *either* male *or* female; it is, not only psychologically or practically, but physically impossible to be both. Nor is the relation of the two sexes to humanity in general like the relation of the different races to mankind as a whole or the relation of the different individual men and women to their race or their nation; it is not simply comparable to the relation of species to genus or of individual to species. It is altogether unique. Humanity—human-ness—can be realized perfectly *either* as masculinity *or* as femininity—as maleness or as femaleness; each is compossible with humanity, they are not compossible in the same individual with each other.

(3) Together with this fundamental alternativity,[5] there is a deep need of the two sexes for each other, both for the enrichment of the lives of individual men and women and for the coherence and the fulfilment of the capacities of mankind as a whole. This far transcends the limits of the merely erotic in the former and of physical maintenance and propagation in the latter. Paradoxically, it is precisely because each sex can realize human-ness only in its own way that it needs the fellowship of the other sex in order to do it. Here I can do no more than outline the situation schematically; what this involves in practice needs for its discernment that deep understanding of the needs and capacities of individual men, women, and children that one finds in the skilled and sensitive pastor and, in a different form, in the great novelist. I have said more upon this point in another place and I will here only repeat one brief passage to rebut a possible misapprehension:

It is very misleading to say, as some do that there are female characteristics in men and male characteristics in women, on the ground that men can be gentle and women can be courageous, for example. I would not admit that gentleness is a basically female virtue, or courage a basically male one. What is true is that there is a male way of being gentle and a female way, and similarly with courage. But heaven defend us from the notion that a man must be effeminate if he is gentle, or a woman masculine if she is brave.[6]

(4) Although there is this fundamental alternativity and complementarity between the two sexes, this does not imply that they are distinguished by nothing but their sheer schematic non-identity, like a geometrical solid and its mirror-image or a right- and a left-handed rotation in mathematics, or like two enantiomorphic crystals or molecules in chemistry.[7] Even on the basic genetic level, they are formally as well as materially different, one consisting of two identical factors (XX) and the other of two diverse ones (XY), and this inherent, and not merely trivial, differentiation permeates every level of their being and activity.

In the light of these considerations we should be able to see the wrong-headedness of the kind of demand for women's liberation that is in effect a demand that women are really men and should be treated as such. It may well be the case that many human societies have been dominated by an implicit or explicit assumption of male superiority and that the social structures, or at any rate those of public life, have been fashioned and developed to correspond with the ambitions, aptitudes, and convenience of men. In so far as this is so—though it ought not to be too readily assumed that facts always correspond to appearances—it is urgently necessary that the structures should be modified, and if necessary drastically reconstructed, so that women and men can play in the whole social fabric—which does not simply mean one dominated by economic and political motives—the parts that are adapted to their several needs and capabilities. What has tended to happen in practice is that women have simply been allowed or encouraged to enter into structures designed for men, and this has largely resulted in women becoming defeminized. G. K. Chesterton once characteristically commented on the admission of women into the business world with the remark that 'twenty million young women rose to their feet with the cry *We will not be dictated to:*

and proceeded to become stenographers.'[8] In fact the admission of women into business was motivated not by any passion for female liberation but by a need for cheap secretarial labour. When quite recently it was conceded that women who were doing a man's job should receive a man's wage, one of the results has been an increased pressure on married women to take paid employment outside their homes in order to counteract the effect on the family budget of the resulting inflation. It would be ridiculous to maintain that the economic problems of the present day are due primarily to the payment of equal wages to men and women, but what is true is that the tendency, which is alarmingly on the increase in democratic capitalist countries, to look upon human beings primarily as producers and consumers of saleable commodities is vastly encouraged by the assumption that women and men are basically interchangeable units and that any ensuing dislocation of family life can be satisfactorily adjusted by a massive substitution of state services for the normal feminine vocations of wife and mother. In fact, the weakness of women's liberation as commonly conceived, as of so many demands for social change whose inspiration is basically secularist, is that it is not revolutionary enough. It attempts to force women into structures which have been designed either simply for men or else without concern for the radical difference between the sexes, instead of reforming the structures in conformity with the nature of the sexes as they truly are. I am not advocating a restoration of the social patterns of the nineteenth century, even were that possible, but they were no more unnatural than are many of the patterns that are advocated by some supporters of women's rights today, encouraged and manipulated as they frequently are by powerful commercial interests. In a situation in which women are, or believe that they are, or can be persuaded that they are, at a disadvantage compared with men, it is fairly easy to produce the impression that to be a woman is an intrinsic disability, the consequences of which can be neutralized only by women making themselves as similar to men as is physically, psychologically, and socially feasible. What is claimed as the liberation of women is in fact their masculinization; the real social inadequacies and injustices are largely ignored and additional ones are inflicted. Space will not allow of a comprehensively illustrated account of this tendency, but I will adduce one example, that of a widespread and energetically propagated attitude to pregnancy, childbearing, and motherhood.

According to this attitude, pregnancy is a tiresome and dangerous disability to which one half of the human race is unfairly subjected and from which the other half is undeservedly exempt. The fact that a great many women welcome it as a wonderful and enriching experience, in spite of the dangers and pains from which even the great advances of modern medicine have not totally freed it, is interpreted merely as a sign that they are still in an immature and servile state of arrested self-realization. Rather oddly, it is hardly ever suggested that the male half of the human race suffers an unfair disability through being deprived of the possibility of this enriching experience. (Even Mr Gore Vidal's Myron Beckinridge couldn't manage to be a mother; and his attempt to change his sex left him unable to be a father either.) The power to bear within one's body and to bring into the world a new human being, so far from being rejoiced in as a wonderful privilege, is presented (and resented) as a tedious and unfair nuisance. In some cases, however, the complaint seems not to be against childbearing but rather against sexuality;[9] this particular aberration reaches an extreme form in the demand of lesbian couples to have children by artificial insemination. This is a typical and outstanding example of the way in which, in an irreligious culture, people complain, however irrationally, about the way in which the world has been made, instead of thanking God that he has made a world at all. 'If only *we* had been allowed to design the human race,' we reflect, 'what a much better method of procreation we should have devised; as it is, we can only make it work tolerably at all by ingenious devices like abortion and sterilization, and even then the remedy is often worse than the disease. Of course, if we believed in God, we should at least be able to blame him for not having made us differently; but then if we really did *believe* in him, we shouldn't be able to *blame* him for anything, should we? Anyhow, we can't blame *ourselves*; we're sinned against, not sinning. It's most frustrating, having a grievance and not having anybody to have it against; there's no satisfaction in having a grievance against the evolutionary process, for it doesn't even know we're having it. . . .'

Is this just a frivolous and fantastic digression? I think not. The point is this. It is right and reasonable to protest when women are unjustly treated, as it is right and reasonable to protest when men are unjustly treated. But what is *just* treatment, of either a woman or a man? It is treating that person in accordance with the nature that she or he has. And while that nature is *human* nature in both, it is radically different in each. There are two ways of being human, male and female; and maleness and femaleness are more than just two superficial or accidental adornments superposed on an undifferentiated human-ness which is qualitatively identical in both. This *alternativity* in human nature belongs to it on all its levels and in all its aspects; we have seen here in some detail how it penetrates to the most fundamental, to that of the genetic constitution. It is relevant to a vast variety of human concerns, among others the violently controverted issue of the Christian priesthood. But now I wish to consider it in relation to the manhood of the incarnate Son of God, our Lord and Saviour Jesus Christ, for this digresson (which has, I hope, not been without its own importance) arose out of the assertion that, if God the Son has become man, then God the Son is incarnable as man and manhood is assumable by God.

SEXUALITY IN JESUS

God the Son, the eternal and consubstantial Word of the Father, through whom all things were made, has become a human being in order to reconcile the whole of mankind to God. (If this was a treatise on redemption, we should have to inquire precisely what this reconciliation involved and whether the Son would have become incarnate if man had not become alienated, but here we need only recognize the simple fact.) He is the universal saviour of mankind; he is also a first-century Palestinian Jew, Jesus of Nazareth. Furthermore, it is not *in spite of* having become one particular human being that he is the saviour of all human beings, but *through* being one particular human being. Nor is it in spite of having become a member of the Jewish people that he has brought into one family all the peoples of mankind, Jewish and Gentile alike, but by having become a member of the Jewish people. I have in a previous chapter devoted some space to this paradoxical but essential union of universality and particularity in the incarnate Lord.[1]

But I have not yet drawn attention to an even more fundamental example of this paradoxical aspect of the incarnation.
Not only is Jesus an individual Jew and as such the saviour of all
mankind, Jews and Gentiles alike; he is an individual male
human being and as such the saviour of all human beings, male
and female alike. This fact needs to be stressed, as it has been
affirmed by some supporters of the ordination of women to the
priesthood that Jesus must have had either the full characteristics of both the sexes or else no sexual characteristics at
all.[2] It must be repeated that to be a human being is to be either
male or female; and God incarnate—God become human
completely and perfectly—must be God who has become a
complete and perfect male or a complete and perfect female.
God incarnate will not be either a hermaphrodite or a eunuch,
but either a man or a woman. And in fact God incarnate is a
man.

Is there, however, any special significance in this? Given the
stupendous decision on the part of God to become incarnate
anyway, does the fact that what was assumed was human nature
as male and not as female amount to anything more than the
fact that if you spin a coin it will come down either heads or
tails, since it cannot come down both at once? In other words,
while the fact that we have a saviour who is God incarnate is due
to an act of overwhelming divine love and compassion, is the
fact that the saviour is a man and not a woman due to
something analogous to mere chance? Many have come near to
suggesting this, in fear that any other answer would imply that
God had favoured one sex—in actual fact, the male—to the
detriment of the other. However, quite apart from a doubt
whether considerations of comparative privilege are relevant in
a matter which is in any case, for both sexes, one of totally
unmerited grace, it is noticeable that this kind of objection has
generally emerged from religious circles which have almost
totally ignored the fact that both sexes have in fact been involved in the incarnation and which now seems to be anxious to
make an attempt at a belated retribution. The human mother
of Jesus was looked upon as a necessary, but otherwise unin-
teresting, mechanism for providing him with a body, and
certainly no special honour was seen as having been conferred
on the female sex by the part which she was called upon to play.
As the Russian Orthodox theologian Dr John Meyendorff has

written: 'There is no doubt in my mind that the Protestant rejection of the veneration of Mary and its various consequences (such as, for example, the really "male-dominated" Protestant worship, deprived of sentiment, poetry and intuitive mystery-perception) is one of the *psychological* reasons which explains the recent emergence of institutional feminism.'[3] In contrast, I would quote words that I have written elsewhere, in which I have emphasized the essential diversity of the two sexes and, in consequence, of the parts which each has played in the central mystery of the incarnation:

> It was male human *nature* that the Son of God united to his divine person; it was a female human *person* who was chosen to be his mother. In no woman has human *nature* been raised to the dignity which it possesses in Jesus of Nazareth, but to no male human *person* has there been given a dignity comparable to that which Mary enjoys as *Theotokos*, a dignity which, in the words of the Eastern liturgy, makes her 'more honourable than the cherubim and beyond comparison more glorious than the seraphim'. In Mary a woman became the mother of God, but to no man, not even to Joseph, was it given to be the father of God; that status belongs only to the Father in heaven. The centrality of womanhood in redemption is shown by the fact that the incarnation itself waited for the courageous and obedient *Fiat* of Mary (Luke 1.38); the initial reaction of the man Joseph, however great his contribution later on, was to be doubtful about his fiancée's chastity (Matt. 1. 18ff).[4]

That the basic difference between the sexes, both in constitution and function, does not imply any inferiority of the female to the male, but rather in some very important aspects a superiority, has been impressively expounded by Père Louis Bouyer, who sets his discussion firmly in a Mariological and ecclesiological content:

> If human *nature* finds its essential and supernatural perfection only in the humanity of Christ, the male prototype of all masculinity, the human *person* finds its initial and unsurpassable perfection in a woman, the Virgin-Mother Mary. And all human persons, saved together, will attain their own perfection only in flowing together into the ultimate per-

sonality of the eschatological Bride, 'the Church of the first-born whose names are written in heaven'. She will have borne them to grace, in the course of the history of salvation, only in order to appear herself, at the end, or rather at the *beyond* of all history, in the glorious virginity of the Bride of the Lamb, come down from heaven from God. [5]

And again:

It is not a fortuitous fact, without importance or significance, that he [sc. the eternal Son] became a man and not a woman and that, in consequence, he associated with his mission apostles of the same sex, a mission which continues down to us by similarly male bishops and priests. . . . On the other hand, it is only from a woman that he could be born among us, as one of us. And if, as St Thomas has made clear, following the whole patristic tradition from St Irenaeus onwards, it belonged to the Virgin Mary, not only to provide him with our flesh, but also to involve the freedom of all mankind in a salvation which would not have been achieved without this, it was not by a meaningless chance that this role fell to a woman and not to a man. [6]

And once more:

What meaning lies in the fact that the Apostles would in vain have been the only official and public witnesses of the Resurrection if the women had not been the first to believe in it! Although they ended up by preaching it to the whole world, their first impression had been that it was silly women's gossip. . . .

It is fully typical of the Church of the Fathers, who confirmed the restriction to males of the apostolic function and the succession to the episcopal and presbyteral functions, that they maintained no less firmly that Mary's vocation, like her holiness, surpassed not only theirs, but even that of the angels most exalted in glory and the most celebrated in their ministry among the elect. [7]

And elsewhere Père Bouyer remarks, commenting on the fact that in the early Church there were official 'orders' of consecrated 'Virgins' and 'Widows', to which there were no male equivalents:

Here, maybe, we have the final clue to the distinctive vocations ascribed to men and to women in the Church from the beginning. The special public vocation of men in the apostolic ministry was seen as a vocation to represent, among all the members of Christ, the Head, a vocation which, like that of the Head itself, belongs to men only. Similarly, the public vocation of women was understood as a vocation to represent the Church as a body, as the Bride of Christ, in its unity as well as in its eschatological integrity. This could be the vocation of women only, as it had been the special vocation of Mary. Once again, *no possible idea of inferiority could be connected with that specialization*, since the Virgin Mary was soon to be considered as higher, in the Church, than the Twelve and St Paul.[8]

Turning now to one of the most brilliant of the younger theologians of the Eastern Orthodox Church, we find in the following passage from the Archimandrite Kallistos Ware the same double emphasis upon the fundamental distinctiveness of man and woman in both the order of creation and the order of redemption:

At his human birth Christ did not only become man in the sense of becoming human (*anthropos, homo*), but he also became man in the sense of becoming male (*aner, vir*). Certainly Christ is the saviour of all humankind, of men and women equally; at his incarnation he took up into himself and healed our common humanity. But at the same time we should keep in view the *particularity* of the incarnation. Christ was born at a specific time and place, from a specific mother. He did not just become human in an abstract or generalized sense, but he became a particular human being; as such he could not be both a male and a female at once, and he was in fact a male.

Secondly, men and women are not interchangeable, like counters, or identical machines. The difference between them, as we have already insisted, extends far more deeply than the physical act of procreation. The sexuality of human beings is not an accident, but affects them in their very identity and in their deepest mystery. Unlike the differentiation betwen Jew and Gentile or between slave and free—which reflect man's fallen state and are due to social convention, not to nature—the differentiation between male and female is an aspect of humanity's natural state before the Fall. The life of grace in the Church is not bound by social conventions or the conditions produced by the Fall; but it does conform to the order of nature, in the sense of unfallen nature as created by God. Thus the distinction between male and female is not abolished in the Church.

We are not saved *from* our masculinity and femininity, but *in* them; to say otherwise is to be Gnostic or Marcionite. We cannot repent of being male and female, but only of the *way* in which we are these things. Grace co-operates with nature and builds upon it; the Church's task is to sanctify the natural order, not to repudiate it. In the Church we are male and female, not sexless. Dedicated virginity within the church community is not the rejection of sex, but a way of consecrating it.[9]

This passage is quoted from an essay in a symposium on the relation of sexuality to the priesthood of the Church, but it is concerned with a principle that logically and theologically precedes that controversial topic. And the production of that symposium was provoked by the conviction, shared by a very varied group of men and women, that it is impossible to discuss satisfactorily whether women can or should become priests unless far deeper consideration is given than has generally been attempted to the question of the signification and purpose of sexuality in mankind as created, fallen, and redeemed. It is not surprising that in the past, when the masculinity of the Christian priesthood has been accepted by a kind of general intuitional consensus, discussion of the reasons for this limitation has tended to be sketchy and superficial. Furthermore, when reference was made to the biological aspects of sexuality, theologians not surprisingly assumed that scientists knew their own business, though the notion that a female was physiologically an imperfect male was enormously counterbalanced in practice by the honour given to Mary in Catholic doctrine and devotion.[10] Embryology has now advanced beyond the stage of Aristotle and this particular point of tension between science and religion has been removed. It is, however, important to recognize that what modern biology has shown, as I have more than once emphasized, is not that the sexes are *identical* but that they are radically *different*. And nowhere is that difference more strikingly manifested than in the distinct but complementary ways in which, according to orthodox Christian belief, masculinity and femininity are involved in the incarnation of the Son of God. Which of the sexes is thereby shown to be the more important could no doubt be argued indefinitely and interminably, and I doubt whether the question has any real significance in a matter wherein both have received privileges of such overwhelming and unforeseeable greatness. God the Son has, through the operation of God the Holy Spirit, become a man by taking human nature from a human mother, and in so doing he has brought salvation and grace to men and women alike. The Son of God, we say, has become the Son of Mary, and we have, it may be hoped, no problem that he is her son and not her daughter. But, leaving the incarnation aside, does it mean anything that he is called *God's* son and not *God*'s daughter? And that God in heaven is described as his Father and not as his Mother? These may be more difficult questions to answer, and some clarification is desirable.

First, we must observe that, although these are distinct questions, since the first question is about the Second Person of the Trinity and the second question is about the First Person, they can hardly be separated, since each involves the relation between the two Persons. *Logically*, however, the answer to the first question might be Yes and the answer to the second question No.[11] Secondly, we must remember that, even when a predicate which generally is applied to creatures can legitimately be predicated of God (as when we say that God is good or wise or just or merciful), it cannot apply to God in the same manner in which it applies to a creature; it must, to use the technical term, be predicated *analogically*. Thus, the application of masculine terms to God does not imply that he has male sexual organs or indeed any physical organs at all; though it cannot be ruled out without further argument that the essential significance of some male epithet may be realized, not just metaphorically, but formally and primarily though analogically,[12] in God.

The first question, then, is this. Does the fact that, when taking human nature, the eternal Word took it as a male imply that the *pre-incarnate* relation of the eternal Word to the first

Person in the Trinity is that of a son and not that of a daughter or (if this is conceivable) that of a sexless offspring? As far as the *incarnate* condition of the Word is concerned, our earlier argument has led us to conclude what the evidence of the Gospels abundantly confirms, that in the realm of the human nature, from the conception in the womb of Mary up to and beyond the glorification of the ascension, Jesus is fully and perfectly a male; and I do not think that anyone has seriously maintained that Jesus was frustrated in the expression of his humanity by the fact that he could not manage to be a woman as well. The most striking expression of Jesus' attitude to God as it is recorded and reflected in the Gospels is that it is one of complete and coequal *filiality*, of filiality involving responsiveness and, in the strict sense, subordination, yet with these no touch of inferiority;[13] and this is filiality in the male and not the female aspect.[14] It is inconceivable, and the Gospels would certainly give no support to the notion, that Jesus was simultaneously the son of Mary and the daughter of God. However, this does not fully answer our question.

SEXUALITY AND GOD

We have accepted the orthodox position that Jesus is the Second Person of the Trinity incarnate in human nature, that *as human* he is both Son of God and Son of Mary, since his life as Son of Mary began when, by the operation of the Holy Spirit, the eternally begotten Word of the Father became in Mary's womb the subject of a human nature. But still the question remains: given that the *filiality* of the Word is pre-existent, is the *maleness* pre-existent as well? Or does a sexually un-differentiated filiality become *son*ship (and not daughterhood) only when it is expressed in a created nature, when the Word becomes flesh and dwells among us?[1] Does maleness, in some archetypal and immaterial mode, belong to the eternal Word even before and apart from the incarnation; or does it commence simply when the human nature commences? In technical terms, does it belong to the *perfectio significata* of the Word's filiality or only to the incarnate *modus significandi*?

If the mere posing of this question should seem to some readers to manifest a pathological case of the academic occupational disease of abstraction and hair-splitting, it must be said that on the answer that is given to it (and to the cognate question about the application of male epithets to the *First* Person of the Trinity) there turns the legitimacy of the traditional language of Christian devotion and liturgy down the ages and, behind that, the language of the New Testament and of Jesus himself. But this is to anticipate. Our present question is this. It is central to Christian orthodoxy that in Jesus filial Godhead is perfectly expressed in human terms through the assumption of human nature by the eternal Word. In him the Word has become flesh, and his glory which we have beheld is glory as of the only-begotten from the Father (John 1. 14); in him the whole fullness of deity dwells bodily (Col. 2. 9). Human nature, as being in God's image, was, in St Thomas's phrase, more 'assumable' than any other; and it was 'highly suitable' that, if any of the divine Persons was to assume it, that Person should be the eternal Word. A number of modern Christologists have held that there is a radical affinity between human nature and the Person of the Word.[2] If this is so, may it not be that not only the humanity of Jesus but also the sexual mode under which he assumed it reflects a real aspect of the eternal Word? Or must we say, on the other hand, that the eternal Word transcends the particularity of his incarnate maleness *in precisely the same way* as he transcends the particularity of his incarnate first-century Palestinian Jewishness?

I have emphasized the words 'in precisely the same way' because, whichever answer we give to this question, there can be no suggestion that either of the sexes is inferior to the other. All creatures are, because of their metaphysical insufficiency and contingency, infinitely inferior to their creator; and all are of amazing dignity and value because they are the objects of his creative power and love. And the limited perfections which they embody are only faint shadows or 'imitations' of the infinite perfection which is God himself. As St Thomas says, 'God is the first exemplar cause of all things';[3] they are 'like' him, though we must not say that he is like them.[4] He is, says the apostolic writer, the Father from whom all fatherhood in heaven and on earth is named'[5]—a very relevant instance here. And it will be well to remind ourselves at this point that the attribution of male epithets to the First Person of the Trinity does not rest upon a very shaky logic based upon the masculinity of Jesus— 'Jesus is male, Jesus is God, therefore God is male; the First Person is God, God is male, therefore the First Person is male'—but upon the way in which God has revealed himself in the concrete historical revelation of Judaism, with its culmination in Christ and its expansion and explication in the worship, thought, and witness of the Church down the ages.

Austin Farrer, in his Bampton Lectures *The Glass of Vision*,[6] maintained the challenging thesis that images have a direct epistemological function, that is to say that they illuminate us directly without the intervention of an intermediate stage of conceptual thought. Just as, in his view, a contemplative metaphysical approach to the natural world can lead by an analogical movement to the God who is its creative ground (this was the thesis of his great book *Finite and Infinite*[7]), so, he held, by living with and feeding upon the great revealed images of the Bible we can be led to knowledge of the supernatural mysteries of the Christian religion. He was emphatic that the biblical images do not function simply in virtue of their natural iconic character as images; they were in fact provided by God to his ancient people the Jews and were taken up, remodelled, fulfilled, and synthetized by Christ, and committed by him to the Church which is his Body for further handling and development. Farrer's insistence on the inspired character of the biblical images and the methodology which he based upon it were very strongly criticized in some circles, notably by Dr T. A. Roberts;[8] the epistemological function of images as such was less widely called in question, and Farrer himself did not restrict it to those that were alleged to be inspired.[9] But in any case it seems difficult for anyone to deny the very special authority of the biblical images if he believes in the uniqueness of the Christian revelation. I will quote at length the impressive and eloquent words in which Farrer describes how the intervention of God in human history appropriates and fulfils the natural imaginings and mythologizings of mankind:

This divine action is the supernatural thing. It is for us as vivid and particular and real a divine action as anything ever conveyed by mythology to a primitive mind. Did God descend from heaven to visit Baucis and Philemon? God visited no less particularly when he entered the virgin's womb. But while Jupiter had only to step down from a definable place above the glassy floor of heaven, the Eternal Word must be gathered from all immensity and begin in

Mary to have a place. Even so to speak is to materialize eternal godhead: immensity is not gathered into Mary, but he who is neither immense nor measurable nor in any way conceivable by spatial extent takes place and body, when the Word of God is made flesh.

The ineffable thing happens: for why should not God do that of which man cannot speak? But man must also speak it; or how shall it be known and believed? Man cannot conceive it except in images: and these images must be divinely given to him, if he is to know a supernatural divine act. The images began to be given by Jesus Christ; the work was continued by the Spirit of Christ moving the minds of the Apostles. It was possible for Christ and the Apostles to use the images meaningfully, because the old archetypes were there to hand, already half transformed under the leading of God in the expectant faith of Israel. Christ clothed himself in the archetypal images, and then began to do and to suffer. The images were further transformed by what Christ suffered and did when he had put them on: they were transformed also by their all being combined in his one person. . . .

The choice, use and combination of images made by Christ and the Spirit must be simply a supernatural work: otherwise Christianity is an illusion. . . .

The Apostolic minds which developed and understood the images of faith performed a supernatural act: but supernatural acts, we remember, are continuous with natural functions, of which they are, so to speak, the upward prolongations. The boundary between the two need be neither objectively evident nor subjectively felt. . . . Such a seizure [sc., by the pentecostal Spirit] was neither the guarantee nor the condition of inspiration: not the guarantee, for compulsive thinking is of itself a purely psychological phenomenon: not the condition, for God can supernaturally mould the thought of the saints apart from it. Inspiration is not a perceptible event.

The images are supernaturally formed, and supernaturally made intelligible to faith. Faith discerns not the images, but what the images signify: and yet we cannot discern it except *through* the images. . . . Have we, outside them, any rule by which to regulate our intuition of what they mean?

Certainly we have a rule, a rule of a highly general kind, in the conception of God supplied to us by natural theology. . . .

Again, within the field of revealed truth, the principal images provide a canon to the lesser images. The reduction of the lesser images to terms of the greater is a theological activity, and we see it already proceeding in him who first earned the title of theologian, the 'divine' St John . . . St John is not reducing everything to a confused simplicity. The images which he 'reduces' to terms of others no more disappear or lose their force, than do the whole body of images, when we remember that they are no more than images, and so reduce them to the one ineffable simplicity of God's saving love. All is denied and all is affirmed. . . .[10]

This is not the place for a detailed discussion of Farrer's epistemology, but I am glad of the opportunity to emphasize the importance of his work and to bring it into the context of our present concern.

Now, in that context it is striking to observe that, with the exception of Maker, which might just possibly be taken as of common gender, all the major images of God which are found in the Bible and are extended into the Church's tradition are of clearly male character—King, Father, Shepherd, Husband, to mention the most obvious. This is significant, because the function of having a variety of representations of any supernatural reality is to prevent an exaggerated emphasis being placed on any one natural analogy and to preserve a balance by reminding us that they are all in their different ways inadequate.[11] In this case, however, if the very notion of maleness as characterizing God were misleading, that deficiency could not possibly be corrected by making use of the whole spread of major biblical images of God, since the character of maleness is common to them all. Unless we are to reject the biblical revelation altogether, may we not be forced to conclude that, in however analogical a way and with whatever reservations about the *modus significandi*, the notion of maleness is appropriate to God in a way that the notion of femaleness is not? And this, in spite of the fact that God, as the creator and exemplar of *all* his creatures, transcends *all* their individual characteristics, material and spiritual, animate and inanimate, rational and irrational, male and female alike?

Dr Gilbert Russell and Dr Margaret Dewey, in a penetrating essay on the psychological aspects of the controversy about the ordination of women,[12] have pointed out that, as a matter of human history, the notion of deity as female has gone together with an absence of the recognition of God as transcendent and with a virtual identification of deity with the immanent forces of nature in the cult of the Earth-Mother. Arguing that, both from the point of view of individual psychology and from that of cultural history, movement from a male to a female archetype is simply regression, they write:

> These human facts are mirrored in our perception of God. He is not, to be sure, either male or female. If he is God, he must transcend all gender. But if he is to manifest himself to his world, still more be incarnate in humanity, it can only be as a male or female person. He chose, as it happened, to manifest himself as male. The reason has been made clear. Most of the ancient world lay in the close embrace of the Earth-Mother, who in her manifold cults was propitiated and honoured simply because all life depended upon her bounty. The great merit of Judaism was that it opposed to this universal cultus the worship of a God whose 'masculinity'— to our eyes often repellent in its aggression and ruthlessness—matched and mastered the compulsive and seductive qualities of the Great Mother. . . . Only the victory of Yahweh over the Earth-Mother could have freed the energies bound up in the yearly 'round' for new social, cultural and religious advance.

To the objection that 'surely we live in a totally different world in which such considerations no longer apply', the two writers vigorously respond:

> We submit that they do. It has yet to be shown that there is, in the field of religion, any alternative to the cult of the Great Father save that of the Great Mother, in one of its many forms. That we, in the western world at least, are moving back into a period of Great-Mother worship is almost too obvious to require demonstration.[13]

I would add only one comment to the impressive argument summarized in these sentences. If, as the writers show, religions that lack a firmly male image of deity lapse into an immanentism in which the sense of a transcendent creator is absent, to say nothing of the corresponding nature and fertility rites with the sexual licence which provoked the denunciations of the Hebrew prophets, is it not likely that the maleness which the Judaeo-Christian tradition attributes to God is more *intrinsic* (if the term may be allowed) to his being and less a matter of mere appropriateness and of arbitrary decision that their language suggests? 'He chose, *as it happened*,' they write, 'to manifest himself as male. The reason has been made clear.' Precisely; but if the reason is as clear as they show it to be, is not the phrase 'as it happened' too weak? Is not the Second Person of the Trinity intrinsically male, as I have argued, whatever is true of the other two? And can we say that the Second Person is intrinsically male without attributing maleness to the other two? To speak in technical terms, is the maleness of the Second Person simply an aspect of his *personal* distinctiveness or is it an aspect of the divine *nature* which is common to all the three?

A hopeful starting point for an answer to this question might be the celebrated Athanasian principle, accepted and amplified by later thinkers in East and West, that all that is said of the Father is also to be said of the Son except that the Son is Son and not Father.[14] It is clear from the context that what is affirmed as peculiar to the two several Persons is simply *derivingness* in the one and *derivedness* in the other,[15] for the whole point of the doctrine asserted is that the Persons are differentiated not by possessing different *properties* but by their mutual *relations*.[16] (This is very clear in St Augustine.)[17] The fact that the Persons are respectively described as the Father and the Son, and not as the Deriver and the Derived, is plainly due to the sound rule of sticking as closely as possible to the language of Scripture and of Christian liturgy and devotion, with its concreteness, familiarity, and emotional warmth. But, if this is so, the element of masculinity that both contain is presumably proper to the Godhead as such; were this not so, we should not have one God in three Persons, but three different Gods with three different natures.[18] And if this is so, then masculinity will apply to the Spirit no less than to the Father and to the Son, although, like intelligence, will, goodness, and personality (in the modern sense of that term)[19] as such, it is not explicitly verbalized.[20]

We must, I think, therefore conclude that the application of

male predicates to God is neither arbitrary nor accidental, but
that its authentication by Scripture and tradition rests upon a
real character of Godhead itself. But in saying this we must be
steadily mindful of the radically analogical nature of all human
concepts when they are predicated of God, and we must
repudiate any suggestion that the female sex is, as such, inferior
to the male. It is perhaps significant that Père Bouyer argues
that the attribution of male epithets to God is not so much an
assertion of masculinity as of fatherhood, and that there is a real
sense in which men are inferior to women, in that a man can
exercise fatherhood only, as it were, by proxy, since unqualified
fatherhood is the prerogative of the Father in heaven, while a
woman can exercise motherhood, as it were, in her own right;
and the actual mechanism of conception and gestation confirms
this. Thus Bouyer writes:

> God, in so far as he is revealed supremely as *the* unique
> Father, appears in certain respects as indeed masculine and
> not feminine: less as *bi*sexual than as *a*sexual, while the
> masculinity of which man himself is susceptible appears in
> him as a characteristic not only derived but borrowed, and
> never capable of entire realization in itself. Even on the
> natural and physical plane, and still more on the super-
> natural, a man can never be a father except, so to speak, by
> proxy, and never is the fulness or even in fact the essence of
> fatherhood present in him. There is only one Father who is
> entirely a father, and this is God. . . .
>
> There is thus, in the masculinity of man, something that
> is not and cannot be complete, and which is genuinely
> complete only in the Son of God made man. And even in
> him masculinity, since it is complete only in the fatherhood
> from which he himself proceeds, to that extent altogether
> surpasses and transcends even divinized humanity. We must
> thus say finally that male man is truly man only in the
> Heavenly Man (I Cor. 15. 45ff), the Son of God, and that
> the only true and integral fatherhood is strictly speaking
> neither masculine nor feminine, since it is the exclusive
> property of the only father who is nothing but father and is
> wholly father, while he realizes equally, in a transcendent
> mode, that virginity of which woman alone in earthly
> humanity can offer some sort of image.[21]

As in all his writings, Bouyer's argument is extremely condensed, and it does not easily lend itself to summarizing. He admits that some of his conclusions are speculative and that his method is largely symbolic. But, he replies, the biblical revelation and the whole sacramental dispensation rest upon the fundamentally symbolic character of creation itself and of human nature in particular. He is content to describe the book from which I have quoted as a 'sketch', while pleading that it should be taken seriously, and this plea is of weight in a subject whose consideration is urgently needed and is almost entirely neglected. He began from a very special question, that of the ordination of women to the priesthood, but he showed very quickly that behind this there lie fundamental issues concerning both the natural constitution of mankind and the inner life of deity itself. No doubt some readers would prefer a simpler approach which made less demands for hard thinking; and if human equality implied human identity that might perhaps do. But if human equality involves diversity rather than identity things will be much more complicated. Among the themes which he investigates are those of the nuptial relation between Jahweh and Israel, of the divine Wisdom, of Mariology and of the Church as the bride of Christ, and it is difficult to see how any of these could make sense if the masculinity of the traditional images of God is discarded as trivial and irrelevant. But I do not know any Christian theologian who so emphatically expounds, without any trace of sentimentality, the dignity—one might almost say the sovereignty—which belongs to the female sex precisely in and because of its difference from the male. Thus he writes:

Man the male, as such, is defined by this paradox, that he essentially represents that which surpasses him, that which he is incapable of being in and by himself, that in which he can share only by sharing through grace in the sonship of the sole eternal Son, who himself represents the Father from whom he proceeds as him from whom everything proceeds; that is to say, God in the inexhaustible vitality of the most absolute transcendence. But, again, on the natural plane, a man can be a father only in a very partial and ephemeral way, while on the supernatural plane he will never represent the divine fatherhood except in dependence on that unique image of the Father who is the sole-begotten Son.

The woman, on the other hand, does nothing but represent the creature in its highest vocation, which unites it with God himself, in his creativity and even in his fatherhood. She is potentially, in her virginity, everything that she represents, and she becomes it in effect in her motherhood when she realizes it in herself. For motherhood is the consummated gathering of all created being, the most intimate and efficacious that can be conceived, into what may be called the very soul of the Godhead, the life-giving, fructifying power of the Spirit. As such it makes possible the most perfect assimilation that there can be of the created to the uncreated, the sharing of divine filiality, in the marriage consummation of the created Bride by her union with the divine Bridegroom. This will be realized in its fulness at the end of time in the Church, as a universal resonance of that which was perfectly accomplished at the centre of time in the virginal motherhood of Mary, a motherhood strictly divine. But this is what every woman for her part, just simply as a woman, if she lives her vocation as a woman, outlines on the natural plane and fulfils on the supernatural, by accepting, like Mary, all God's design for her.[22]

Such a passage as this, taken out of its context, can show no more than one facet of Bouyer's profound and many-sided thought. And neither he nor I would claim that he has said the last word on this urgent but neglected matter. What I think one is entitled to hold is that it is totally superficial to discard or depreciate, as explicable simply by linguistic usage or cultural context, the traditional masculine terms in which the Church has described her God. But at the same time it is essential to stress that this does not imply any inferiority of women to men, even when the word 'subordination' is used. For it is often forgotten that *sub-ordination* in the strict sense, that is to say the placing of some persons under the direction of others for certain purposes, applies not only to the relation between the sexes but to any structured and orderly human society. Dr Margaret Hewitt has pointed out that the assertion of the Apostle in I Cor. 11 that man is the head of woman, as Christ is the head of man and God is the head of Christ, in no way implies inferiority, since Christ is not inferior to God the Father but is equal to him, as the only-begotten and eternal Son.[23] This will of course mean nothing to those who deny the deity of Jesus. But this just shows how important orthodoxy is.

Notes

Foreword

1 *The Future of Belief, Theism in a World Come of Age* (London, Burns & Oates, 1967), 92; discussed in my *Openness of Being* (London, Darton, 1971), ch. 8.
2 Cf A. D. Galloway, *Wolfhart Pannenberg* (London, Allen & Unwin, 1973), 94f.
3 *Man, Woman and Priesthood*, ed. Peter Moore (London, SPCK, 1978), 9ff.
4 *Soul Friend* (London, Sheldon Press, 1977), 35f.

CHAPTER 1
Man and His Mind:
The Defence of the Intellectual Principle

WHATEVER HAPPENED TO THE HUMAN MIND?

1 *The Spirit of Thomism* (New York, Kenedy, 1964), 42. But this is not an exclusively Thomist doctrine.
2 B. Russell, *Human Knowledge: its Scope and Limits* (London, Allen & Unwin, 1948), 196; *Outline of Philosophy* (London, Allen & Unwin, 1927), 302.
3 *The Metaphysical Foundations of Modern Physical Science* (London, Kegan Paul, 1932), 227. Ironically, Newton himself never recognized how deterministic his system was: ibid., 280ff. Cf my *Secularisation of Christianity* (London, Darton, 1965), 195f.
4 *English Philosophy since 1900* (OUP, 1958), 112.
5 Ibid., 113.
6 Professor W. H. F. Barnes, strangely for a First in Mods and Greats, uses the form *'sensibilium'* (*The Philosophical Predicament*, London, A. & C. Black, 1950, 72)!
7 *A Treatise of Human Nature*, I, iv, 2 (Everyman ed., London, Dent, n.d., I, 200).
8 *History of Philosophy* (Boston, Ginn, 1903), 520.
9 Op. cit., I, iv, 7 (ed. cit., I, 254).
10 *An Outline of Philosophy* (London, Allen & Unwin, 1927), 83.
11 Cf Warnock, op. cit., ch. vi.
12 Ibid., ch. iv; cf E. L. Mascall, *Words and Images* (London, Longmans, 1957), ch. 1.
13 Cf Warnock, op. cit., vi. For a more detailed account of some aspects of this movement, cf J. O. Urmson, *Philosophical Analysis: its Development between the two World Wars* (Oxford, Clarendon Press, 1956).
14 Dr Arthur C. McGill has written, in an article on Anselm's Ontological Argument:

   That language is merely derivative and expressive is an axiom inherited from the seventeenth century. . . . For the rationalistic philosophers, clear and distinct ideas were somehow produced in the mind directly by reality, without any mediation of language. . . .

Today, for the first time in centuries, a serious challenge is being raised against this subjectivistic theory of language. Words, according to Martin Heidegger, are not primarily the tools by which men express what is already in their heads. Rather they are the *instruments of reality itself*, the medium through which being discloses itself, using man's voice as its spokesman. Language is not about reality, it is reality in the state of unveiledness, and in every statement it is the subject matter—not the subjectivity of the author—which addresses man's thought [Recent Discussions of Anselm's Argument, in John Hick and Arthur McGill edd., *The Many-Faced Argument* (London, Macmillan, 1968), 110].

It will be seen later on (pp. 21ff) that I do not accept either of the views which McGill here sets in contrast regarding the relations of language, the mind, and reality. I quote him here, however, simply for his account of Heidegger.

15 *Philosophical Investigations* (Oxford, Blackwell, 1953), I, 126.
16 London, Allen & Unwin.
17 I have, for example, made no mention of the immense practical influence of Gilbert Ryle, whose famous work *The Concept of Mind* (London, Hutchinson) appeared in 1949, or of dissidents such as A. N. Whitehead, A. C. Ewing, and Professor J. N. Findlay.
18 Cf my *Christian Theology and Natural Science* (London, Longmans, 1956), 80ff.

THE ROAD TO RECOVERY

1 I take this example from *Christian Theology and Natural Science*, 239.
2 *Infallibility: the Crossroads of Doctrine* (London, Sheed & Ward, 1977), 153.
3 *Christian Theology* . . ., 49.
4 Ibid., 82f; cf ch. 2 *passim*, 'The Nature of Scientific Theories'.
5 Louvain (1922–47), 5 vols., largely published posthumously.
6 *Le point de départ* . . ., V, *preambulum*; cit. *A Maréchal Reader*, ed. and trans. J. Donceel, S.J. (New York, Herder, 1970), 65.
7 *The Transcendental Method* (New York, Herder, 1968), 67.
8 Cf E. Gilson, *Réalisme thomiste et Critique de la connaissance* (Paris, Vrin, 1939); J. Maritain, *The Degrees of Knowledge*, 2nd E.T. (London, Bles, 1959), ch. 3 (French original *Distinguer pour unir*, 4th ed., Paris, Desclée 1946).

INTELLIGENCE AND INSIGHT

1 London, Longmans.
2 London, Darton.
3 London, Darton (1971), chs 4, 5.
4 London, Darton (1976), ch. 1.
5 Cf my *Nature and Supernature*, 10f.
6 London, Darton (1968).

7   *Insight*, 635.
8   This passage is reproduced, with slight changes, from *The Openness of Being*, 84f.
9   *The Openness of Being*, 85ff; *Nature and Supernature*, 20ff.
10 *Method in Theology*, 55 *et al.* The fourth maxim hardly appears in *Insight*.
11 I believe that this diagram accurately represents Lonergan's terminology. It is, however, my construction from his writings, not his.
12 Cf my *Nature and Supernature*, ch. 1; *Theology and the Gospel of Christ* (London, SPCK, 1977), 56f.
13 London, Burns & Oates (1967).
14 *Theological Studies*, XXVIII (1967), 336ff, reprinted in *A Second Collection* (London, Darton, 1974), 11ff.
15 Hugo Meynell, 'Lonergan's Method: its Nature and Uses', in *SJT*, XXVII (1974), 162ff.
16 *S. Th.*, I, xvi, 1c; *De Ver.*, i, 2 sed contra 2; cf *S.c.G*, I, lix.
17 *The Degrees of Knowledge*, ed. cit., 87, n.1.
18 With some hesitation, I use 'reality' rather than 'thing' to render the Latin *res*, since 'thing' has in English a suggestion of vagueness as well as of limitation to non-living beings. I do not, however, intend 'reality' as an abstract noun, like the Latin *realitas*, but as thoroughly concrete and definite.
19 *S. Th.*, I, lxxxvii, 1 *ad* 3.
20 Cf, as one example, the rearguard action fought by Mr (now Sir Alfred) Ayer in the two editions of *Language, Truth and Logic* (London, Gollancz, 1936, 1946).
21 Heidegger apparently held some such view as this; cf p. 9, n. 14 *supra*.

MIND AND REALITY

1   *Evolution in Action* (London, Penguin, 1963), 36.
2   *The Openness of Being*, 25.
3   Ibid., 27.
4   Ibid., 28.
5   Opening speech of the Second Vatican Council, 11 October 1962, Walter M. Abbott, ed., *The Documents of Vatican II* (London, G. Chapman, 1966), 715.
6   'Pluralism in Theology and the Unity of the Creed in the Church', *Theological Investigations* XI (London, Darton, 1974), 3ff (date of original 1969).
7   'Pluralism and the Unity of Faith', *Method in Theology* (London, Darton, 1972), 326ff.
8   London, Sheed & Ward (1977).
9   Op. cit., 290.
10 Ibid., 319, n. 9.
11 *The Future of Belief*, 92.
12 *The Times*, Monday, 18 July 1977.

CHAPTER 2
On from Chalcedon

IS CHALCEDON RELEVANT TODAY?

1   This impression is much reinforced by Professor G. C. Stead's very detailed study *Divine Substance* (Oxford, Clarendon Press, 1977).
2   It is irrelevant whether Chalcedon was correct in supposing that 'the Symbol of the One Hundred and Fifty' was composed and ratified by the Council of Constantinople of A.D. 381; cf J. N. D. Kelly, *Early Christian Creeds* (London, Longmans, 1950), ch. 10.
3   *Foundations*, by Seven Oxford Men (London, Macmillan, 1912), 230.
4   *Christus Veritas* (London, Macmillan, 1924), 134.
5   Loc. cit., n. 5.
6   Cf, e.g., E. C. S. Gibson, *Thirty-nine Articles*, 3rd ed. (London, Methuen, 1902), 536, n. 1.
7   London, Methuen (1903 and many reprints).
8   London, Black (1958), Preface, p. v. Cf p. 338: 'The Chalcedonian Settlement'.
9   London, Hodder (1966), 9.
10   Cambridge, C.U.P. (1967).
11   London, SPCK.
12   *Introduction à la théologie chrétienne* (Paris, Seuil, 1974), 272.
13   *Le Fils éternel* (Paris, Cerf, 1974), 403ff.
14   *Jesus der Christus* (Mainz, Matthias-Grünewald, 1974); E.T. *Jesus the Christ* (London, Burns & Oates, 1976), 239.
15   Washington, D.C., Corpus Books (1969); there is a French version, *Le Christ dans la théologie byzantine* (Paris, Cerf, 1969).
16   Chicago, Univ. of Chicago Press (1974), especially ch. 2.
17   Op. cit., 3.
18   Cf Bouyer, op. cit., 404; Meyendorff, op. cit., 53ff.

JESUS HUMAN AND DIVINE

1   Op. cit., 57, corrected from French version.
2   Ibid. In saying that the hypostasis is 'ontologically distinct' from the divine nature, Meyendorff of course does not mean to suggest that it could ever be ontologically *separated* from it. In view of the fact that, as Meyendorff points out (op. cit., 52), the phrase 'crucified God' can be found in as orthodox a father as St Gregory Nazianzen, Dr J. Moltmann's choice of it as a title for one of his recent books (London, SCM, 1974) need not have seemed so novel as has been generally thought.
3   Cf W. Kasper: 'Since the oneness of God and man, as it occurred in Jesus Christ, cancels neither the distinction between them nor the autonomy of man, but realizes that oneness and that distinction, reconciliation occurs in Jesus as liberation, and liberation as reconciliation—at one and the same time. Here God is not, as modern atheistic humanism asserts, a restriction but the condition and basis of human freedom. Christology can approach and tackle the legitimate concern of the modern era and resolve its problem.' (*Jesus the Christ*, London, Burns & Oates, 1976, 16)
4   *The Humanity and Divinity of Christ* (Cambridge Univ. Press, 1967), 106.

5 Ibid., 67. (italics mine)
6 *The Remaking of Christian Doctrine* (London, SCM, 1974), 54, 38 *et al.*
7 'The Christ of Christendom', in John Hick, ed., *The Myth of God Incarnate* (London, SCM, 1977), 140.
8 *The Month*, CCXXXVIII (1977), 111ff.

THE FIRST-CENTURY JEW THE UNIVERSAL SAVIOUR

1 Cf their contributions to John Hick, ed., *The Myth of God Incarnate* (London, SCM Press, 1977).
2 If Aquinas is correct, there is an even more extreme case, that of the angels, in which each individual forms a separate species; cf *S. Theol.*, I, l, 4. In any case, there can be only a still more distant analogy between the *logical* particularization of the species in the individual and the *theological* particularization of human nature in Jesus through its hypostatic union with the creative Word.
3 London, Black, Dacre Press, 3 vols. (1950, 1952, 1956).
4 Op. cit., vol. I, 1ff.

THE CONDITIONS OF JESUS' MANHOOD

1 I have discussed the character of this recognition in my book *Theology and the Gospel of Christ* (London, SPCK, 1977), 137, 167ff, *à propos* the Christology of L. Bouyer and J. Galot.
2 *Le Fils éternel: Théologie de la Parole de Dieu et Christologie* (Paris, Cerf, 1974), 476.
3 'Current problems in Christology', in *Theological Investigations*, I (London, Darton, 1961), 168. The original, in German, was written not later than 1954.
4 Ellen Flesseman-van Leer, 'Dear Christopher, . . .', in M. Hooker and C. Hickling, edd., *What about the New Testament?* (London, SCM Press, 1975), 239f.
5 Liam Walsh, OP, *Summa Theologiae*, Blackfriars ed., XLIX (1974), 84f.
6 I would not now suggest, however, as I did in 1946 (*Christ, the Christian and the Church*, London, Longmans, 56ff), that there is a *direct* infusion of knowledge into the human mind of Jesus from the person of the eternal Word who is its metaphysical subject; and I do not think that most conservative Christologists at that time would have suggested it either.
7 Op. cit., London (SPCK, 1977), 131ff, 195ff.
8 The old distinction between the supernatural *quoad substantiam* and *quoad modum* may be useful here, but it supplies the framework rather than the answer for the questions involved. Cf Additional Note C *infra*.

CHALCEDON IN A WIDER CONTEXT

1 Presses de Taizé (1962).
2 *Lumen Gentium*, cap. 6: 'The Role of the Blessed Virgin Mary, Mother of God, in the Mystery of Christ and the Church'.
3 At the present time, in some quarters of the Roman Communion the reaction has gone so far that devotion to Mary has become virtually non-existent.

4   *L'Orthodoxie*, Neuchâtel, Delachaux (1959), 113, my italics.
5   London, Darton (1966), 91ff.
6   *The Phenomenon of Man* (London, Collins, 1959), 297.
7   Kenelm Foster, OP, *Summa Theologiae*, Blackfriars ed., IX (1967), xxi, my italics.
8   London, Darton (1964).
9   'One Jesus, many Christs?', in S. W. Sykes and J. P. Clayton, edd., *Christ, Faith and History* (Cambridge Univ. Press, 1972), 142.
10 'The Outcome: Dialogue into Truth', in John Hick, ed., *Truth and Dialogue: The Relationship between World Religions* (London, Sheldon Press, 1974), 151.
11 'Epilogue', in John Hick, ed., *The Myth of God Incarnate* (London, SCM Press, 1977), 202.
12 London, Longmans (1956), 36ff.
13 Op. cit., 44. Cf the tentative remarks of Dr C. F. D. Moule, *The Origin of Christology* (Cambridge Univ. Press, 1977), 143.
14 Ibid., 45.

ADDITIONAL NOTE A: *Incarnation and Sonship*

1   London, SPCK (1977), 137, 162.
2   *Le Fils éternel* (Paris, Cerf, 1974), 510.
3   *La Conscience de Jésus* (Gembloux, Duculot; and Paris, Lethielleux, 1971), 90f.
4   *New Fire*, IV (1977), 463.
5   *The Brink of Mystery* (London, SPCK, 1976), 20.
6   London, Longmans (1956), ch. 2.
7   Art. cit., 468.
8   Ibid.

ADDITIONAL NOTE B: *Dr Moule on the Origin of Christology*

1   London, SCM.
2   Op. cit., 3.
3   Ibid., 18.
4   Ibid., 19.
5   Ibid., 77f.
6   London, Faber. A 'Revised Review' by Dr Moule appeared in *Theology*, LXIV (1961), 144ff.
7   Op. cit., 80.
8   Ibid.
9   Cambridge University Press.
10 Op. cit., 1.
11 John Hick, ed. (London, SCM, 1977).
12 Op. cit., 2f.
13 LXXVI (1973), 562ff, 573ff; LXXVII (1974), 404ff.
14 Op. cit., 138.
15 Ibid., 53.
16 Ibid., 142.
17 Cf my *Christian Theology and Natural Science* (London, Longmans, 1957), 36ff, 311ff.

ADDITIONAL NOTE C: The Shroud of Turin

1   Kenneth Stevenson, ed. (Holy Shroud Guild, 294 East 150 Street, Bronx, N.Y. 10451, 1977).
2   LXXX, 193ff.
3   Xavier Rynne, *Letters from Vatican City* (London, Faber, 1963), 99.
4   London, Hodder (1978).
5   14/21 April 1979.

CHAPTER 3
Suffering and God: Passion, Compassion, and Impassibility
CHANGE AND BECOMING: FR WEINANDY'S ANALYSIS

1   Cf p. 33 *supra*; also the discussion of Père J. Galot's Christology in my *Theology and the Gospel of Christ* (London, SPCK, 1977), especially pp. 162ff.
2   *Theology and the Gospel of Christ*, 179n, 183n, 201.
3   Ph.D. thesis, University of London, 1975. I quote from this by courtesy of the author. Cf his article 'Aquinas and the Incarnational Act: "Become" as a Mixed Relation', *Doctor Communis*, Vatican City, XXXII, 15ff.
4   Op. cit., 96f.
5   Ibid., 82f.
6   *S. Th.* III, i, 1 ad 1.
7   Op. cit., 120f.
8   *S. Th.* III, ii, 7 ad 1.
9   Op. cit., 122.
10 Ibid., 122f.
11 This is a slip; Weinandy should have written 'objects of knowledge would not in reality be known'. The object of knowledge, not the knower, is the logical term in the relation of knowing.
12 Op. cit., 124.
13 Ibid., 125
14 Ibid., 127f.
15 Ibid., 128. It is not, of course, meant that *all* mixed relations are creative.
16 Ibid., 129f.
17 Ibid., 130.
18 Ibid., 131.
19 Ibid., 132f.
20 Ibid., 134.
21 Ibid., 134f.
22 Ibid., 135.
23 Ibid., 141f. Leontius of Byzantium rather than Leontius of Jerusalem in fact!
24 Ibid., 151.
25 Ibid., 157.
26 Ibid., 154.
27 Ibid., 160.
28 Ibid., 173.
29 Ibid., 181.
30 Ibid., 184.

31 Ibid., 187.
32 Ibid., 193.
33 London, Sheed & Ward (1972).
34 Weinandy, op. cit., 195.
35 Cf p. 32, *supra.*
36 Schoonenberg, op. cit., 74.
37 Ibid., 87.
38 Op. cit., 200.
39 London, Darton (1961–).
40 Weinandy, op. cit., 203.
41 *The Trinity* (London, Burns Oates, 1970), 85ff.
42 Op. cit., 205.
43 Rahner, *Theol. Inv.* I, 181n; cf IV, 113.
44 Op. cit., 212. Cf Y. Congar: 'May we not try to overcome the antinomy in terms of grace? God is grace, because he is love. In these conditions, may we not suppose in God, in his very being, the capacity to be the subject of a story in another? For God is the subject of a story of which all the mutability resides in the other, but of which God is truly the subject. He can do this in so far as he is grace, for in this way he is not only in himself but in another. When St Thomas, in the first article of the Third Part, seeks the intelligibility of the Incarnation in the idea of the *bonum diffusivum*, he is not acting otherwise' (Comment on Rahner in *Problèmes actuels de Christologie*, edd. H. Bouëssé and J.-J. Latour (Paris, Desclée, 1965), 403f).
45 Op. cit., 213.
46 Pp. 151–188.
47 *Theology and the Gospel* . . ., 183.
48 Op. cit., 214.
49 Ibid., 215.
50 Ibid., 217.
51 Ibid., 218.
52 Ibid.
53 Cf p. 71 *supra.*
54 Gembloux, Duculot (1971), 75ff.
55 Gembloux, Duculot (1969), *passim.*
56 Op. cit., 221.
57 Ibid., 219f. It is essential to recognize that 'potency' in this passage means passive potentiality, not active powerfulness as usually in modern speech.

SOME FURTHER CONSIDERATIONS

1 Cf p. 95 *infra.*
2 *Existence and Analogy* (London, Longmans, 1949), 116.
3 *The Openness of Being* (London, Darton, 1971), 27. I sometimes wonder whether the apparently ineradicable 'logical paradoxes' do not owe their obstinacy to the fact that logic, when it ceases to be an instrument used and controlled by real intelligent beings to understand a real intelligible world but is sent out to operate on its own, becomes ultimately a self-devouring chimaera.
4 There are, of course, other AMRs than creation and incarnation, e.g.

divine premotion, which establishes the freedom of the will, and grace, which directs the intellect and the will of rational creatures to their supernatural end.

5 William and Martha Kneale, *The Development of Logic* (Oxford, Clarendon Press, 1962), 25.

6 Not to be confused with the five 'predicables': definition, genus, difference, property, and accident.

7 *De Trinitate*, V, v. Cf my *Theology and the Gospel of Christ*, 214f.

8 *La Personne du Christ*, *passim* discussed at length in my *Theology and the Gospel of Christ*, 151ff.

9 The relevance of this distinction may be more obvious in the case of polyadic relations, i.e. relations that unite more than two terms, typically $R(a,b,c, . .)$; I have suggested elsewhere that their theological exploration might be fruitful (*Theology and the Gospel of Christ*, 230f). The Easterns hold that the Son and the Spirit severally proceed from the Father by the two distinct processions of generation and spiration, fGs and $fSsp$, while the Westerns hold that the Spirit proceeds from the Father and the Son, *tamquam ab uno principio* $(fGs)Ssp$. Might the recognition that the three Persons are mutually, and each in his own proper manner, held together in one embracing relation of divine life $T(f,s,sp)$, offer a starting-point for reconciliation? May this not be a legitimate development of the doctrine of *perichoresis* or circumincession?

10 These typical sentences, from Leontius of Jerusalem and St Gregory Nazianzen respectively, are quoted by Dr John Meyendorff in *Christ in Eastern Christian Thought* (Washington, D.C., Corpus Books, 1969), ch. 4.

11 Rom. 8.26.

12 *Process and Reality* (Cambridge U.P., 1929), 497.

13 *Concepts of Deity* (London, Macmillan, 1971), 24.

14 Ibid., 24f.

15 New York, Herder; London, Burns & Oates (1968–70).

16 Op. cit., II, 404; reprinted without bibliography in K. Rahner, ed., *Encyclopaedia of Theology* (London, Burns & Oates, 1975), 577.

17 Ibid.

18 Ibid.; *Encyc.*, 578.

19 Ibid., 405; *Encyc.*, 579.

20 Ibid.

21 Ibid., 406; *Encyc.*, 580.

22 Ibid.

23 OUP (2nd ed. 1974), edd. F. L. Cross and E. A. Livingstone, 694.

24 Paris, Lethielleux (1976).

25 *Theology and the Gospel of Christ*, 151.

BEING AND LOVE: FR GALOT'S APPROACH

1 Op. cit., 9.

2 Ibid., 11.

3 Ibid., 25.

4 Ibid., 32.

5   Ibid., 41f.
6   *Theology and the Gospel of Christ*, 184.
7   Cf my *Theology and the Gospel of Christ*, 136f, 150, 161ff.
8   Op. cit., 55.
9   Ibid., 56.
10 Ibid., 60.
11 Ibid., 63.
12 Ibid., 150.
13 Ibid., 154f.
14 Ibid., 160.
15 Ibid., 161.
16 *S. Th.* I, xix, 2, 3; *S.c.G.* I, lxxvi, lxxx, lxxxi.
17 Op. cit., 161.
18 Ibid., 166.
19 Ibid., 167.
20 Ibid., 190f.
21 K. Rahner, *The Trinity*, 86f; Galot, *Dieu souffre-t-il?*, 63ff.
22 I would stress the word 'rightly' here. I would maintain that our use of
    temporal language to speak about eternal realities is not only inevitable
    but is also, when understood analogically, entirely legitimate. Cf the
    chapter on 'God and Time' in my book *The Openness of Being* (London,
    Darton, 1971), especially pp. 165ff.
23 As by J. A. T. Robinson, *The Human Face of God* (London, SCM,
    1972), ch. 5; G. W. H. Lampe, *God as Spirit* (Oxford, Clarendon,
    1977), ch. 5, where the traditional doctrine is carefully expounded and
    then rejected. Cf pp. 112ff, *infra*.
24 *The Openness of Being*, 173.
25 *Via Media: an Essay in Theological Synthesis* (London, Longmans, 1956).
26 Op. cit., xiii.

CHAPTER 4
Quicunque vult . . . .? Anglican Unitarians

DR LAMPE'S BAMPTON LECTURES

1   *Theology and the Gospel of Christ* (London, SPCK, 1977), 121.
2   G. K. A. Bell, *Randall Davidson* (London, OUP, 1935), ii, 872.
3   S. W. Sykes, *The Integrity of Anglicanism* (London, Mowbrays, 1978),
    21.
4   London, SCM (1977).
5   Cf my discussion of the symposium, op. cit. *supra* 202ff.
6   Essay in *Christian Believing* (Report of the Doctrine Commission of the
    Church of England) (London, SPCK, 1976), 126.
7   *God as Spirit* (Oxford, Clarendon Press, 1977), 228.
8   *God as Spirit*, 1. Subsequent references to this work are given in
    parentheses in my text.
9   *The Origin of Christology* (Cambridge Univ. Press, 1977), 138.
10 *The Remaking of Christian Doctrine* (London, SCM, 1974), 38.
11 *Chance and Necessity* (London, Collins, 1972), 49 *et passim*.
12 Cf their contributions to *The Myth of God Incarnate* (London, SCM,

1977) and my criticism in *Theology and the Gospel of Christ*, 202ff.

13 Cf W. Pannenberg, *Jesus God and Man* (London, SCM, 1968), *passim*.

14 Cf A. D. Galloway, *Wolfhart Pannenberg* (London, Allen & Unwin, 1973), 96 *et alibi*.

15 *The Logic of Gospel Criticism* (London, Macmillan, 1968), 185. For a discussion of this important work, cf my *Theology and the Gospel of Christ*, 82ff.

16 1 Cor. 15. 14–17.

17 Cf: 'We may, *if we wish*, call this contemporary indwelling divine presence "Christ"' (loc. cit., my italics). This, we are told, among other advantages, will prevent us from 'leaving the Christ-event behind us altogether' and from 'ceasing to recognize the Spirit of God as the Christ-Spirit and the effect of his indwelling presence as Christlikeness'.

18 G. W. H. Lampe and D. M. MacKinnon, *The Resurrection* (London, Mowbrays, 1966).

THE SURVIVAL OF THE TRIUNE GOD

1 Cf review of *God as Spirit* by A.E.H. in *New Fire* V (1978), 40f.

2 Cf V. Lossky, *The Mystical Theology of the Eastern Church* (London, James Clarke, 1957), ch. 3; J. Meyendorff, *Byzantine Theology* (London, Mowbrays, 1975), ch. 14; *et al.*

3 For a moderately expressed example, cf Lossky, loc. cit.

4 *The Trinity* (London, Burns & Oates, 1970), 83f. Cf his 'Remarks on the dogmatic treatise "De Trinitate"', *Theological Investigations* IV (London, Darton, 1966), 77ff. The latter is much the more readable in the English translation.

5 J. Meyendorff, *Christ in Eastern Christian Thought* (Washington, D.C., Corpus Books, 1969), 165f.

6 Dante, *The Divine Comedy*, tr. Dorothy L. Sayers and Barbara Reynolds (Harmondsworth, Middx, Penguin Books, III, 1962), 346.

7 Matt. 5. 8.

8 Lossky himself admits this of Cistercian mysticism, especially of William of St Thierry (*Mystical Theology of the Eastern Church*, 65, n. 1).

9 *Mystical Theology of the Eastern Church*, 65.

10 *The Doctrine of Sacrifice deduced from the Scriptures* (1879), xii, cit. A. R. Vidler, *The Theology of F. D. Maurice* (London, SCM, 1948), 34f.

11 Cit. A. M. Allchin, *The Spirit and the Word* (London, Faith Press, 1963), 51.

12 Cit. Stephen Yeo in M. B. Reckitt, ed., *For Christ and the People* (London, SPCK, 1968), 15.

13 *The Trinity*, 101ff. I think also that he makes unnecessarily heavy weather with the term 'person', but I suspect that complications of the German language may lie behind this.

14 Eph. 3. 5, 2. 18, 1. 10.

15 *Religious Language* (London, SCM, 1957), ch. 2; *Models and Mystery* (London, OUP, 1964), ch. 3.

16 Cf my *Existence and Analogy* (London, Longmans, 1949), *passim*.

17 Cf S. L. Jaki, *The Relevance of Physics* (Chicago Univ. Press, 1966), 74ff; E. Whittaker, *A History of the Theories of Aether and Electricity*, I (2nd ed. 1951), London, Nelson, esp. chs 9, 10.

18 London, Hutchinson (1959).
19 *Theological Science* (London, OUP, 1969).
20 *Theological Investigations*, IV, 98.
21 Even Fr Rahner professes himself as uneasy with the trinitarian ap-
    plication of the term 'person', in view of its modern connotations, and
    expresses a preference for 'distinct manner of subsisting', while
    disowning Karl Barth's term 'manner of being' (*The Trinity*, 108ff; cf
    Theological Investigations, IV, 101f), though because of its traditional
    status he does not propose to abandon it. I myself find it difficult to
    worship a manner, however distinct it may be or of whatever it may be
    the manner.
22 Cf *O.D.C.C.*, London, OUP (2nd ed. 1974), 295; G. L. Prestige, *God in
    Patristic Thought*, London, SPCK (2nd ed. 1952), xxxiii, 291ff.
23 J. Galot, *La Personne du Christ* (Gembloux, Duculot, and Paris,
    Lethielleux, 1969), ch. 2, esp. 31, 41. He also suggests the usefulness of
    the term 'hypostatic relation' as avoiding a possible ambiguity in 'sub-
    stantial relation'. For a discussion of his very illuminating use of the
    notion in Christology, cf my *Theology and the Gospel of Christ*, 151ff.

CHAPTER 5
Sexuality and God

INTRODUCTION

1 Cf J. N. D. Kelly, *The Athanasian Creed* (London, A. & C. Black, 1964),
   19f.
2 The *Quicunque* also makes brief mention of the union of soul and body
   in each man as an analogue or image of the union of divinity and
   humanity in Christ. The limitations and dangers of the analogy have not
   gone unnoticed; its use is to show that there can be a union of two
   distinct elements which is more than trivial or accidental.
3 Ch. 2, pp. 38ff, *supra*.
4 L. Bouyer, *Le Fils éternel* (Paris, Cerf, 1974), 421; K. Rahner, *The
   Trinity* (London, Burns & Oates), 1970, 85f; E. L. Mascall, *Theology and
   the Gospel of Christ* (London, SPCK, 1977), 147.
5 *S. Theol.*, III, iii, 5, 6, 7.
6 Ibid., iii, 8; iv, 1.
7 Ibid., iv, 1 ad 2. St Thomas even suggests that *angelic* nature might be
   'assumable' in principle, though this would be 'incongruous because
   unnecessary', since all actual angels are already either saved or damned.
   And I do not think that the Angelic Doctor ever asserts that God ever
   does anything that is in fact 'unsuitable' (*inconveniens*).

SEXUALITY IN MAN

1 Good popular accounts are not, however, difficult to find, e.g. ch. 16 of
   Anthony Smith's *The Body* (London, Penguin, 1974).
2 Op. cit., 275. I have discussed the highly special case of the virginal
   conception of Jesus in *Theology and the Gospel of Christ*, 131ff.
3 'Only one characteristic is known to be linked with the Y chromosome
   apart from maleness,' wrote Anthony Smith in 1974, 'and that is "hairy

ear rims'' ' (op. cit., 303). One more has been reported since.

4   Various views are held about the way in which the sex-chromosomes influence each other. At the time of writing (October 1978) the dominant view appeared to be that the Y interferes with the natural tendency of the X to produce a female, and, by stimulating the appropriate hormones suppresses the growth of female characteristics and promotes the growth of male ones instead. To say, as in *The Times*'s Science Report of 19 October 1978, 18, that 'in a sense male development can be viewed as a perturbation of the natural development of the embryo into a mature female', when in fact the 'perturbation' is a normal process, suggests the smuggling of an evaluative judgement into what is supposed to be an objective scientific description. The 'possible exception' mentioned in the text is that of a rare abnormality in which, it is alleged, a mutation on the X-chromosome of an XY cell has given the X-chromosome a resistance to the inhibiting influence of the Y partner, so that, although the individual's genetic composition is XY and therefore male, the entire development and functioning is that of a female. Dr Neill Spencer tells me in a letter of a condition, 'testicular feminization', in which by a biochemical abnormality (roughly 1 case in 20,000) the testes produce female rather than male hormones in a XY individual, and that similarly many 'apparent males' are XX. He adds that infrequently a binucleate egg may be fertilized by two sperms, an X and a Y, producing what is called a chimera.

    Such admittedly abnormal cases, whatever problems they may posit for the pastoral and moral theologian, and however their purely biological assessment may be modified by future research, do not affect the judgement expressed in the text.

5   Note that I write 'alternativity', not 'alternation'. By 'alternativity' I mean that a human being is *either* male *or* female irrevocably, not sometimes one and sometimes the other or possibly both at once or something in between. Even 'sex-change' operations and sex-hormone treatments, whatever their physiological and psychological effects, do not alter the basic genetic constitution.

6   'Some Basic Considerations', in *Man, Woman and Priesthood*, ed. Peter Moore (London, SPCK, 1978), 21.

7   A mathematical comparison may illustrate this point. The two square-roots of −1 (which are logically isomorphic with right- and left-handed rotations) have entirely identical properties, in that no descriptive definition can be given of one which will not apply equally to the other; in this they differ from the two square-roots of + 1, which can be distinguished as the one which is identical with the original number and the one which is not. Nevertheless the two square-roots of −1 are not identical with each other, for each is the negative of the other. It may be added that the two portions of the famous Chinese Yin-Yang symbol, which have been associated with the two sexes, do not provide an example of this and are therefore inappropriate. They are not mirror-images of each other but are straightforwardly congruent to each other in the same plane, though they fit together to make up a circle. Nor are they formally different, like the human sex-chromosomes. They are thus

doubly inadequate as a representation of human sexuality, though they might serve for certain asexual worms, which propagate by the conjugation of two similar individuals.

8   Maisie Ward, *Gilbert Keith Chesterton* (London, Sheed & Ward, 1944), 178f, quoting *via* Christopher Morley.

9   I remind the reader that I use the word 'sexuality' to mean not eroticism but simply the differentiation of human beings into male and female.

SEXUALITY IN JESUS

1   Cf pp. 38ff, *supra*.

2   A variant of this second view appears to be that Jesus had physical male characteristics but that they were entirely irrelevant to the rest of his human make-up. It is difficult, however, to believe that the holders of any of these views have thought out their implications at all thoroughly.

3   *The Orthodox Church*, September 1975, p. 4, cit. Kallistos Ware in *Man, Woman and Priesthood*, 78.

4   *Man, Woman and Priesthood*, 23f.

5   *Mystère et ministères de la femme* (Paris, Aubier, 1976), 62f. There is a shorter essay by Père Bouyer, 'Christian Priesthood and Women', in *Man, Woman and Priesthood*, 63ff.

6   Ibid., 69f.

7   Ibid., 71f.

8   *Man, Woman and Priesthood*, 65 (my italics).

9   'Man, Woman and the Priesthood of Christ', in *Man, Woman and Priesthood*, 81f.

10 St Thomas touchingly remarks that one reason why it was fitting that Christ should take flesh from a woman was that it abolished any excuse for despising the female sex (*S. Theol.*, III, xxxi, 4 ad 1).

11 There was a catch question about a fat and a thin German who were walking together down a street in Cologne. The thin German was the son of the fat German; what relation was the fat one to the thin one? Everyone replied that he was the thin German's father, but the correct answer was that she was his mother.

12 I have piled up these adverbs deliberately, to exclude a merely univocal understanding.

13 On the point that Jesus was uniquely conscious not simply of God but of God as his co-equal Father, since it was not simply God but the Person of God-the-Son that had become man in him, cf my *Theology and the Gospel of Christ*, 137, 161f.

14 'Filiality', without qualification, could include both son (*filius*) and daughter (*filia*).

SEXUALITY AND GOD

1   This is a suitable point at which to remark on the irrelevance of arguments based simply on the grammatical gender of words in various languages. The most traditional theologians, writing in a Romance language, will use, without any suggestion of femaleness, feminine nouns and pronouns for, e.g., 'person' or 'Trinity'. (*La personne de Jésus-Christ . . . elle*', '*la sainte Trinité . . . elle*', etc.) Cf the fact that

'Spirit' is masculine in Latin, feminine in Syriac, and neuter in Greek. When William Temple in 1917 entitled a book *Mens Creatrix*, he was not arguing for a female deity. But the story of the French author who began a dedication '*A la Très Sainte Trinité: Madame . . .*' may be apocryphal. We may recall the anecdote of the Englishman at a banquet, who, having drawn his French neighbour's attention to an insect by the warning '*Le mouche*' and received the polite correction '*La mouche, monsieur*', replied in surprise, 'You must have very good eyesight!'

2 Cf my *Theology and the Gospel of Christ*, 149.

3 *S. Theol.*, I, xliv, 3.

4 *S. Theol.*, I, iv, 3 ad 4.

5 Eph. 3. 15.

6 London, Dacre Press (1948).

7 London, Dacre Press (1943, 2nd ed. 1959).

8 *History and Christian Apologetic* (London, SPCK, 1960).

9 Cf my *Theology and Images* (London, Mowbray, 1963), 3f, from which the last sentences are mainly taken.

10 *The Glass of Vision*, 108ff.

11 As with the various 'theories of redemption'; cf p. 124, *supra*.

12 *Man, Woman and Priesthood*, 91ff.

13 Op. cit., 95.

14 Athan., *3 c. Arianos*, 4: 'Since they are both one in essence and divinity, it follows that whatever can be affirmed of the Father may as truly and properly be affirmed of the Son, except only the relation of Fatherhood.'

15 A full trinitarian discussion would have to include the Third Person with the other two but the present point would not be affected. Generally it may be said that the East, with its rejection of the *Filioque*, sees the distinctiveness of the Son and the Spirit as arising from the fact that they proceed from the Father by two different *kinds of derivation*, while the West sees it as arising from the fact that they proceed from two different *origins*, the Son proceeding from the Father alone, while the Spirit proceeds from the Father and the Son together, acting as one principle. Nevertheless, the West denotes the two processions by two different names, 'generation' and 'spiration' respectively.

16 Of course, in a secondary and largely linguistic sense, to-be-in-a-particular-relation may itself be conceived as a 'property'. This is the basis of St Thomas's doctrine of the *notiones* in the Trinity: *S. Theol.*, I, xxxii, 2–4.

17 *De Trin.*, v, 5.

18 This will hold whether we adopt the 'Eastern' attitude (exemplified in the Nicene Creed) that the 'One God' is archetypally the Father, while the Son and the Spirit are God by derivation from him, or the 'Western' attitude that the one God is the Self-existent Being, who is internally differentiated into the three Persons. (The geographical allocation of these attitudes needs considerable qualification.) Fr Karl Rahner has shown sympathy for the 'Eastern' approach: *Theological Investigations*, I (London, Darton, 1961), 79ff.

For a fuller exposition of the doctrine of the Person as *substantial*

171

relation or *relational being*, cf my *Theology and the Gospel of Christ*, 152ff.

19 It should be stressed that 'personality', in the *descriptive* sense in which it denotes a divine attribute (as when, for example, it is said 'Christians believe in a personal, not an impersonal deity' or 'God may be more than personal, as we know personality, but he cannot be less') is an aspect of the divine *nature* and is common to the three Persons because of their common divinity, while the function of their denomination as Persons in the *theological* sense is not to characterize their common possession of divinity but to emphasize their diverse modes of possessing it; St Thomas frankly faces the question whether in fact the three Persons can all be called 'persons' (*S. Theol.*, I, xxx, 3). And, as regards the application of the concepts of intelligence and will to characterize the respective processions of the Son and the Spirit, a distinction is drawn between the 'essential' and the 'personal' use of names (I, xxxiv, 1; xxxvii, 1).

20 It has often been remarked that, in Christian liturgy and devotion, direct addressing of the Spirit is rare, though its presence is as significant as its rarity. Forced attempts to readjust this are, in my opinion, misjudged, as there are good reasons for it. The Father is made known to us through the Son, and the Son is made known to us by the Spirit, but there is no fourth divine Person to make the Spirit known; he is the *locus*, as the Son is the *agent*, rather than the object, of divine revelation. Just as the pattern of divine activity in creation is *from* the Father *through* the Son and *in* the Spirit, so the pattern of the creature's response is *to* the Father *through* the Son and *in* the Spirit. The Spirit is experienced by us rather like the air which we breathe, by his effects, rather than like a visible external object. The classical Western shape of liturgical prayer is offered to the external Father 'through Jesus Christ our Lord [his] Son, who lives and reigns with [him] in the unity of the Holy Spirit, God for ever and ever.' (Eastern formulas, which begin by addressing the Father but end as an ascription of praise to the Trinity, manifest an orthodox reaction to Arian and similar heresies.)

21 *Mystère et Ministères de la Femme*, 34ff.

22 Ibid., 47f.

23 *Christian World*, 2 November 1978, 11.

Index of Proper Names